ENDORSE

M000280927

Jeremiah Johnson's book *Houses of Glory* is both a refreshing and a convicting read. My heart leapt as I envisioned the Houses of Glory that Jeremiah prophesied regarding. My spirit releases a hearty, resounding *"Yes"* to the Lord, and I know you will too. And as always, Jeremiah presents thought-provoking communication that invites all who read to deeply seek and inquire of the Lord.

PATRICIA KING
Minister, author, television host

I believe we are in the midst of one of the most significant transitions in human history, and it's one that will culminate with the return of our King Jesus. God is shaking everything that can be shaken and is calling us to build in such a way that isn't destroyed by the increasing glory and shaking. Wineskins are changing. Structures are changing, and the Holy Spirit is shouting to the Church to "wake up" and come into alignment with what heaven is doing. This is why I am so grateful for this book. In an hour where many are declaring everything is going to be fine, God is raising up prophetic voices like Jeremiah to call us prepare both individually and corporately for what is coming. *Houses of Glory* is a gift to the church in this hour, and I believe it has the potential to shift us and prepare us to thrive in the midst of the coming Glory and Shaking.

COREY RUSSELL
Author and Speaker
Author of *Glory Within* and *Teach Us to Pray*

Fair warning, if you're looking for an ear tickler, this is not it! Jeremiah Johnson's latest book, *Houses of Glory,* boldly confronts the systematic dysfunction that has often hindered the Body of Christ. It is especially relevant for those of us that are ministers and leaders in the church. If you will humble yourself and allow the Holy Spirit to speak through these pages, I believe you will be convicted, provoked, and ultimately greatly encouraged to fulfill your calling and live a life worthy of it.

EVANGELIST DANIEL KOLENDA
Christ for All Nations
President/CEO

What you hold in your hand is a book that carries incredible wisdom for this new era. Jeremiah has penned in these pages keys that are crucial for the Body of Christ in navigating and understanding this new era.

These pages are dripping with the anointing that brings truth, revelation, purity, alignment, direction, clarity, hope, and faith to position you and prepare you for the days we are in. This is a "keep going back to" book for this new era. What a gift this book is to the Church!

LANA VAWSER
Lana Vawser Ministries
Author of *The Prophetic Voice of God, A Time to Selah,* and *I Hear the Lord Say New Era*

We are living in one of the most unique times in human history. Never has there been a greater need for a clear prophetic message to come from the church than at the present moment. God is raising up a new breed of prophetic ministry that will prophesy truth without regard for the intimidations of men nor the oppressions of the enemy. Jeremiah Johnson is one such voice. In his book, *Houses of Glory: Prophetic Strategies for Entering the New Era,* he emphasizes many of the important issues relevant for our day including the great need for a pioneering anointing to be released to lead us into the long foretold new day. I believe those that read this book will gain valuable insight into God's heart for this hour and a greater ability to position themselves for this new journey in God.

PAUL KEITH DAVIS
WhiteDove Ministries

Houses OF Glory

DESTINY IMAGE BOOKS BY JEREMIAH JOHNSON

Judgment on the House of God

The Power of Consecration

Cleansing and Igniting the Prophetic

Wisdom Builds the House
Prov 24:3

Houses
OF
Glory

PROPHETIC STRATEGIES FOR
ENTERING THE NEW ERA

JEREMIAH JOHNSON

© Copyright 2021–Jeremiah Johnson

All rights reserved. This book is protected by the copyright laws of the United States of America. This book may not be copied or reprinted for commercial gain or profit. The use of short quotations or occasional page copying for personal or group study is permitted and encouraged. Permission will be granted upon request. Unless otherwise identified, Scripture quotations are taken from the NEW AMERICAN STANDARD BIBLE®, Copyright © 1960, 1962, 1963, 1968, 1971, 1972, 1973, 1975, 1977, 1995 by The Lockman Foundation. Used by permission. Scripture quotations marked KJV are taken from the King James Version. Scripture quotations marked NIV are taken from the HOLY BIBLE, NEW INTERNATIONAL VERSION®, Copyright © 1973, 1978, 1984, 2011 International Bible Society. Used by permission of Zondervan. All rights reserved. Please note that Destiny Image's publishing style capitalizes certain pronouns in Scripture that refer to the Father, Son, and Holy Spirit, and may differ from some publishers' styles. Take note that the name satan and related names are not capitalized. We choose not to acknowledge him, even to the point of violating grammatical rules.

DESTINY IMAGE® PUBLISHERS, INC.

P.O. Box 310, Shippensburg, PA 17257-0310

"Promoting Inspired Lives."

This book and all other Destiny Image and Destiny Image Fiction books are available at Christian bookstores and distributors worldwide.

Cover design by Eileen Rockwell
Interior design by Terry Clifton

For more information on foreign distributors, call 717-532-3040.

Reach us on the Internet: www.destinyimage.com.

ISBN 13 TP: 978-0-7684-5733-9
ISBN 13 eBook: 978-0-7684-5734-6
ISBN 13 HC: 978-0-7684-5736-0
ISBN 13 LP: 978-0-7684-5735-3

For Worldwide Distribution, Printed in the U.S.A.

1 2 3 4 5 6 7 8 / 25 24 23 22 21

DEDICATION

To the pioneers and trailblazers of this new era, may we honor those who have gone before us and impart hope and courage to those who come behind us.

CONTENTS

FOREWORD

$\mathcal{W}$e are living in an extraordinary time in history. Things are shifting dramatically as the nations of the earth have been shaken in unprecedented ways and hearts everywhere are longing for answers. It is astonishing to see how much chaos and confusion has swept across our land. We find an accurate description of our time in Isaiah 60:2: *"For behold, darkness will cover the earth and deep darkness the peoples."* Yet, the prophecy doesn't stop there. *"But the Lord will rise upon you and His glory will appear upon you."* Throughout church history and even in our own age, dark times always precede a fresh outpouring of God's glory.

In his new book, Jeremiah Johnson aptly writes that in the midst of global crisis, the stage is being set "for the end-time Church to arise with glory and splendor."

Opportunities to advance the Kingdom of God are opening up in manifold ways as the Church walks into the new era that has begun in the spirit. As followers of Christ, we need to prepare for what God is getting ready to release into our nation and into our generation.

Jeremiah Johnson is an amazing prophetic voice from the younger generation, and the Lord has given him profound insight into the times and seasons we are in. Spiritual discernment is necessary for the Church to take action according to how the Spirit of God is moving on the earth today (see 1 Chron. 12:32). Jeremiah continues to release timely prophetic words that I believe will strengthen and encourage the Body of Christ and America in this hour.

Houses of Glory: Prophetic Strategies for Entering the New Era is a book that will help to equip the Body of Christ with a biblical framework for Spirit-empowered ministry in the 21st century. Through his unique perspective, Jeremiah Johnson shares from his prophetic journey to encourage those who are seeking God's will for their lives and desire to step into their God-given calling. He offers a candid appeal to join the move of the Spirit while relying on the strong foundation of God's Word, which is essential for effective ministry to take place.

God's original blueprints for His *Ekklesia* (Church) are being restored as believers all around the world are discovering the value of the fivefold ministry, with renewed emphasis on the role of apostles and prophets (see Eph. 2:20). This is part of the new wineskin that God has prepared for the Church. Spiritual fathers are also taking their place to foster the move of God and speak destiny into the sons and daughters. No matter your age or vocation, it is time for us as Christians to embrace the fresh vision that is being released and learn how we can partner with Heaven in our own spheres of culture. Our potential and influence are maximized whenever we turn to God's solutions for the problems that we face in society.

God is on the move. And His people are coming together in greater unity, purity, and power than ever before. It is my prayer that this book will spark the fires of revival within you, as we anticipate a greater outpouring of glory unlike anything the world has ever seen!

CHÉ AHN
Founder and President,
Harvest International Ministry
Founding and Senior Pastor,
Harvest Rock Church, Pasadena, CA
International Chancellor, Wagner University
Founder, Ché Ahn Ministries

Special Introduction

I, along with many other prophetic voices, have been proclaiming that we have entered into a *new era* and that there are *new ways* for the new era. In fact, on Passover evening of April 2020, as the global pandemic was climbing to its height, I was worshiping the Lord alone late at night in my backyard. The voice of the Lord clearly came to me saying, *"I have been waiting for such a long time for My people to slow down long enough to hear what I have to speak to them. For I have much that I want to speak to them about the new ways for the new era, about the new wineskins for the new wine. I want to speak to them about seed time and harvest, and those who have sowed in tears will be among those who will reap with great joy. Will you be like Moses and turn aside? I am waiting there."*

As you read this book by one of God's new young champions of the faith, you will notice that even the title of the book reflects the very essence of the word the Lord spoke to me on that infamous Passover evening. *"I want to speak to them about the new ways for the new era, about the new wineskins for the new wine."* Amazing, isn't it? It is like Jeremiah and I are listening to the same Holy Spirit!

I also find it interesting that Jeremiah Johnson chose Ché Ahn, founding apostle of Harvest International Ministries, to compose the foreword for this unique book and asked me to write a special introduction. That is unusual to have both us doing introductory material for the same book. That could come across as rather repetitive or unnecessary. But what is even more interesting is that I have served with Ché Ahn as a prophet, to him as an apostle, for well over twenty-plus years. So here we are, having modeled for years elements of what Jeremiah is declaring and contending for in his generation—things like integrity, accountability, relational and positional authority, church planting, new wineskins, and how character really matters!

I will pray at nighttime and ask the Lord to speak to me in my dreams. Many of you know that the Holy Spirit regularly speaks to me in the night season through dreams and visions. So I inquired of the Lord what He wanted me to say about Jeremiah Johnson and this particular book. So, once again, our faithful God came through. In the early hours of the morning I was awakened by the voice of the dove of God. *"Tell them about the three Cs. Yes, I am looking for people who carry the three Cs, and My servant, My friend Jeremiah carries these three Cs."*

So of course, I responded with all ears and an inquiring heart, *"What are the three Cs?"* Quickly an answer came to me: *"I am looking for carriers of the three Cs: Content, Character, and Charisma. These carriers will not bypass the work of the Cross of Christ. These carriers will carry their cross and die to self every day."*

You can always tell when you have heard God. God's thoughts are higher than your thoughts and God's thoughts stick with you long after your thoughts fleet away. So here you go with a special introduction for a new era book containing old ways made new for such a time as this! Well done, Jeremiah. Well done, Holy Spirit!

Blessings to each of you!

JAMES W. GOLL
Founder of God Encounters Ministries
GOLL Ideation LLC

Chapter 1

THE GLOBAL SHAKING

*D*uring the writing of this book, COVID-19 is ravaging the nations of the earth. World economies and entire continents have shut down in an attempt to stop the spread of the virus and find a cure. On June 25, 2020, Robert Redfield, Director of Disease Control said, "We have all done the best we can do to tackle this virus, but the reality is that it has brought the nations to their knees."[1] I have never witnessed so much confusion, shock, fear, and uncertainty in all my life. However, my greatest surprise and heartache in the midst of the pandemic has actually come concerning the Body of Christ. It appears that we, the global Church, have also been brought to our knees as the barrage of deception, division, and conspiracy theories have increased at an unprecedented level. The need for truth, sobriety, and biblical theology regarding the house of God and the end times has never been greater.

The global shaking happening in our world today is seriously revealing our foundations in the Church. The torrent of spiritual and physical storms that are crashing upon the shores of America and other nations are simply exposing the type of house we have chosen to build in the Church and even our personal lives. We must remember that one of the outstanding biblical principles that Jesus taught in Matthew 9 was that He will not fill what He Himself has not formed. He will not put new wine into old wineskins (see Mark 2:22). In other words, are we crying out for God to fill up a last-days wineskin in the Church that He actually has no interest in filling, and is COVID-19 making that answer very clear? The disillusionment, questions, and opinions surrounding where the global Church goes from here are astounding.

One night as I was preaching during the pandemic, I received a shocking open vision and was startled by what God said and revealed to me in that moment. He began.

> *I am releasing judgment upon the Church because of her pulpit idolatries and the hirelings who have filled My house. For even now, I am stripping them of their wealth, titles, and*

desires to be worshiped. Many churches and hirelings will never recover after the virus has lifted because of My judgment. For I will expose the false prophets and priests in the land who feed themselves and not My sheep. Oh, how My heart breaks for the lost sheep who are not being taught how to feed on My word and worship Me. Rather, they are being falsely deceived into man worship, which is idolatry. Repent of celebrity Christianity and recognize the window of time I have now opened for a divine reset in the global Church, says the Lord.

I want to be very clear and make sure the reader does not misunderstand this encounter. God did not say that COVID-19 is judgment upon the global Church. Rather, He is communicating to us that during the time of the pandemic, He is releasing a cleansing judgment upon His house that is intended to prepare us for one of the greatest outpourings of the Holy Spirit that we have ever witnessed. In the following pages, we will begin to address some of the issues God spoke to in this open vision, but the greater aim is to articulate an apostolic blueprint and prophetic strategies so that houses of glory might be established as we enter into a new era in the Body of Christ. It is vital that we recognize prophetically that the coronavirus has given the global Church a divine opportunity to shift and make very significant changes as we enter the new era in the global Church.

CRISIS OR REVIVAL

One of the most frequent questions Christians around the world feel the need to ask concerning the last days is regarding whether they will be filled with crisis or revival. Before answering that I would like to pose a more revealing question. Why is it necessary to choose one or the other? My answer is simply *both*. Both crisis and revival will mark the last days, but the underlying desire in the global Church to have one without the other has seriously crippled our foundations and paved the way for unbiblical theology and an unprepared Bride to face an hour of crisis such as COVID-19. Mike Bickle speaks into this issue with wisdom and experience as he shares:

> I have found in over 40 years of teaching on the end times that preaching on revival is what the people crave the most but it only produces temporary change in their lives. However, when teaching on the crises that will mark the end times, I have discovered it most often produces sobriety and alertness long term.[2]

THE PERFECT STORM

In 2015, I had a life-changing prophetic dream that I believe speaks to the current crisis and even prophesied about it in many ways. In the encounter, I found myself standing on the shoreline of the Atlantic coast facing the ocean. There was a tremendous storm front that was beginning to gather in the Atlantic. I could see the tip of Florida to my right and the upper parts of Maine to my left. I had a sense that I was somewhere near or in Virginia.

As I looked up over the Atlantic Ocean, I noticed two enormous storms beginning to form. The first front moved ahead of the other. The Spirit of God spoke to me and said, "The Perfect Storm is upon America." These two fronts immediately began to move toward me, and demons began to manifest inside of them. I called out to the first front sweeping toward me and said, "Who are you?" The word "Rebellion" flashed before my eyes. I called out to the front behind it and said, "Who are you?" The word "Tolerance" appeared in the sky.

As these tremendous storms now passed over my head, I violently cried out and said, "I live in the most rebellious and tolerant generation that the world has ever known." The Spirit of God responded to me and said:

> *The former prophets looked for physical storms by which they saw My judgments coming, but in these days I'm raising up prophets who will discern spiritual storms. You must know that the spiritual storms that are upon the earth are far greater than any physical storm that has touched earth. Physical storms are limited to a region of people. These spiritual storms that shall rise in the earth will have the power to affect every area of culture. Beware!*

As I faced America on the Atlantic coast and saw these two massive storms sweeping the land, I felt the tremendous urgency of the hour. I immediately jumped on a horse and began to ride, and the word "Paul Revere" was placed in my mouth as I rode. During the next years in the dream, I traveled to different churches all over America proclaiming what I had seen and heard. Though I went to thousands of different churches and visited numerous ethnic groups all over America, there were only three categories of churches. The following are the encounters that I had as I visited the different churches.

THE SLEEPING CHURCH

The first type of church I visited had "Sleeping Church" engraved on its doors. As I opened the doors to these churches, every one of them was in the middle of a service. I would hurry in to relay the message of what I had just seen and heard, only to be shocked to see everyone in attendance, including the leadership, sucking on pacifiers. While this type of church could hear my words, they had no ability to respond. I began to cry out and say, "Why are you silent, Church, why are you silent? Though you are awake, you are sleeping!"

In the dream, the Holy Spirit immediately spoke to me Ephesians 4:14: *"Then we will no longer be infants, tossed back and forth by the waves, and blown here and there by every wind of teaching and by the cunning and craftiness of people in their deceitful scheming"* (NIV). In Revelation 3:1, Jesus rebuked the church at Sardis and told them they had the appearance of being alive, but really they were dead. Be on the lookout for churches in America given over to an entertainment spirit who are spiritually immature. It appears that they are thriving due to the volume of programs, but from heaven's perspective they are lethargic and infantile.

THE STREET CHURCH

The second type of church I visited met in the streets of America. Upon seeing all of these different gatherings in many different cities, I was delighted because many of them seemed to be around my age (18 to 35) and simply claimed allegiance to "Street Church." I began to interview and ask members of this particular type of church if they had heard about the two storms descending over America named "Rebellion" and "Tolerance." None of them seemed to understand what I was asking.

I continued in the street on my horse until I found myself at a gathering of thousands and thousands of these "Street Church" people. They were protesting and filled with anger. As I pressed into the crowd, there was an incredible sense of chaos and confusion among the people. Many began to riot, burn buildings, and loot stores. I cried out to the Lord in the dream and said, "Who are these people?" He said, "These are the products of the works-based Gospel movement of the '80s and '90s. These are they who have rebelled in the name of grace but not in the name of My Son." As the Spirit spoke this to me, there began to be mass commotion in the crowd. They started looting and rioting in many major cities.

Suddenly, banners began to be carried by the Street Church all over America that read "GRACE." It was especially intriguing to me that these banners were dusty, and you could visibly see the mud on them. I said to the Lord, "Where have these young people picked up these banners from?" He said, "They have resurrected them from the former generations. False doctrines that were once done away with are now rising in the streets. Universalism, humanism, and denying the existence of hell will overtake many young people."

After visiting these two types of churches, I was in great distress. I cried out to the God and said, "Take me to Your church." I immediately rode up on a church building that had "Surrendered Church" on its doors.

THE SURRENDERED CHURCH

I quickly walked in and sat down. I immediately noticed that in the back of this church was a gaping hole. It was as if a blast had gone off and almost entirely knocked out the back walls of the Surrendered Church. As I visited Surrendered Churches all over America, I found the exact same thing. I sat in the back and asked the Father what had happened. He said, "My church was at first deceived by rebellion and tolerance. The Street Church you just saw stormed out of the back of My church and left because of the lack of foundation and character, but now My church has been awakened and shall be repaired."

I got up out of my seat and watched as many people were working on repairing the gaping hole in the back of the church. As I watched, I noticed something interesting; the workers were not just any workers. They were true apostles and prophets restoring the foundation, and many of them were teaching other young people how to properly lay the foundation. Meanwhile, many intercessors were in great travail repenting but having a great sense of hope as they cried out and thanked the Father for awakening His Son's Bride from deception and for restoring the foundation layers to His Church.

The Perfect Storm has landed in America and Rebellion and Tolerance have swept over our land. Rioting, looting, and misguided anger are threatening to destroy businesses and churches. Entertainment churches have an appearance of being filled with life but really, they are spiritually dead. Three different types of churches are on every street corner in America. Will the Surrendered Church arise and take its rightful place among the masses?

I knew by way of this revelatory dream in 2015 that we would see a tremendous increase of tolerance and rebellion in America. I now recognize that COVID-19 has simply just ripped off the band-aid of a drowning culture in deep need of an encounter with Jesus Christ. I'm now prophesying and warning you that one of the greatest challenges that the Church in the West is facing and will face is how to deal with young people who have never understood or been taught biblical grace that brings true freedom from sin. Many of these individuals have been overly exposed to legalism and because of this are now embracing false grace and unbiblical views on love. They will walk in a lawless spirit and speak out openly against any kind of authority. They are being influenced by an anti-christ agenda and many of them don't even know it. As we enter into the new era beyond the COVID-19 pandemic, will the Surrendered Church arise full of glory and sobriety?

THE DIVINE RESET

From a redemptive perspective, what if COVID-19 has helped to facilitate a desperately needed divine reset in the global Church? What if in the time of silence (quarantine) God is seeking the spiritually violent? What if it's time to get back to prayer and the Word of God and put all our church growth textbooks and ideologies back on the shelf? What if crisis is actually creating the correct climate in the earth for the end-time Church to arise with glory and splendor? The tares are being separated from the wheat in this time of harvest and we must seek to build God's house His way with greater intentionality than ever before. We must love the truth at all costs and not get swept away in end-time deception. Will the Surrendered Church emerge like I saw in my dream? What might the role of apostles and prophets be in the divine reset?

I believe a fresh generation of young and old trailblazers are being called forth right now. It's time for the firebrands to arise and begin to build a house of glory for the Lord. These vessels of honor aren't rising to establish a "new normal" but rather they will restore the ancient foundations that Jeremiah and Isaiah saw. Holiness and the fear of the Lord still matter. Revival is going to come to many lost young people who are being positioned for a divine encounter from above.

These pioneers will build according to the pattern that Paul and the apostles received from Jesus Christ Himself. It's time to look toward the future with the hope and confidence that can only be found in Jesus's promise when He said, "I will build My Church, and the gates of hell will not prevail against it" (see Matt. 16:18). Our Bridegroom King seeks a glorious and spotless Bride who is geared for emergency. A remnant is rising who will not run away from the coming battle lines but rather run straight for them. To the true Church of Jesus Christ—this is your finest hour. Now is the time to arise and shine, not run and hide. You were born for such a time as this. If your heart is hungry for an apostolic blueprint and prophetic strategies concerning houses of glory that will thrive in the midst of global crisis, keep reading!

NOTES

1. Amanda Holpuch, "Coronavirus has brought US 'to its knees', says CDC director," The Guardian, June 23, 2020, https://www.theguardian.com/world/2020/jun/23/anthony-fauci-covid-19-statement-house-hearing.
2. Mike Bickle, "Positive Trends, People, and Events in the End Times," February 17, 2007, https://mikebickle.org/watch/mb_1378.

Chapter 2

THE CALL TO PIONEER

*H*aggai cried out to his generation, *"Is it time for you to live in luxurious houses while the house of the Lord lies in ruins?"* (See Haggai 1:4.) The prophet's passion and plea with the people around him could have only come from God Himself, because the call to pioneer will cost you everything. We live in a time and period in the earth when many take their liberty to point out what's wrong with the house of God, its leaders, and all of its short-comings. In fact, the truth is that I have never met more people who could accurately identify what's wrong with the Church and who are also simultaneously unwilling to do anything about it than now. However, I believe you picked up this book because you are called to be an activist, critical thinker, and revolutionary pioneer as we enter this new era.

Over a decade ago I was apprehended by the Spirit of God sitting in the back of a church conference on the last row. "You are going to plant a church called, 'Heart of the Father Ministry.'" Like a lightning bolt shot from the sky, I fell out of my chair during worship and began to weep in agony. I remember so clearly saying, "Oh God, I will do anything, anything, just please do not ask me to plant a church." My deep groans and travail came from a sincere heart who was not naïve to the price that is required to actually build a house of glory for the Lord. As a father in the faith once said to me, "Any donkey can kick down a barn, but it takes a wise master builder to establish one." In other words, it takes no skill or prophetic gift to call out the sin and shortcomings of the house of God, but it does take wisdom, grace, and tremendous sacrifice to pioneer a house of glory.

We learn from the Old Testament that when the work of the Lord is suspended, delayed, or perhaps even going in the wrong direction, God raises up prophets like Haggai and Zechariah to prophesy and stir up the spirit of Zerubbabel in the land. We are at a very critical time in history when I believe God is raising up prophets to actually call upon apostles and pioneers to build houses of glory in the earth that can thrive in the midst of global shaking. Prophetic strategies are being released to the end-time Church that will assist us in fulfilling this precious mandate. This is why so many of you picked up this book. God is calling you right now to begin to either build a house of glory or actively assist a group of people in doing so in your city. We can no longer just offer our opinions or even accusations from the sidelines of our various comforts and conveniences. We must begin to act, support, and even finance the work of the Lord in our midst.

MY JOURNEY IN CHURCH PLANTING

Through my own personal experiences, I want to share some of my journey with you as I sought to build a house of glory for the Lord. Far from perfect, the early years were especially painful and full of mistakes. By detailing our story, I hope to impart hope and courage to an emerging generation of pioneers both young and old. Here is a recent and very detailed journal entry I wrote several weeks ago as I was prayerfully remembering those days.

> When we planted Heart of the Father Ministry, we had no "interest meetings" (not sure what those are), we had no launch team assembled, no space for a nursery or kids' church, and we didn't even have words or a projector for the

worship songs. Did I mention we had no budget? I began attending every church planting seminar and conference I could, only to realize that 99 percent of them were trying to teach me how to become a CEO of an enterprise and develop a church model that could not be found anywhere in the New Testament.

I met with over 25 pastors and leaders that first year who told me I was way too young and inexperienced, encouraged me to take out loans to pay for everything, wait until I had a 10-year plan, or go get more education. After meeting with several close friends who nearly convinced me I had not heard from God, I remember weeping on my floor in a state of desperation and helplessness. God spoke a word to my heart from Isaiah 66:9 that literally sustained me the first year of the church plant. It says:

"Shall I bring to the point of birth and not give delivery?" says the Lord. "Or shall I who gives delivery shut the womb?" says your God.

I am forever indebted to the grace of God and several key fathers in my life who encouraged and helped me through those first five years of believing God for the impossible and watching Him move in crazy ways every time. One thing I know through planting a church with simply a word from God is this: God's will *is* God's bill! He is so faithful. We were in five different buildings in five years and God just kept moving. He brought the most quality Christian families and people I have ever met in one city. There were days when I was so discouraged and ready to quit, but He met with me in my despair and in my mistakes. Honestly, I look back on our church planting journey and feel the deep need to ask many people for forgiveness whom I'm sure I hurt in the process of trying to figure it all out. Planting a church is the single hardest thing God has ever asked me to do.

In 2016, after Jericho marching (literally) a million-dollar facility in Lakeland, Florida for 21 days with fasting and, again, believing God for the impossible, He answered! We purchased a beautiful church building all to God's glory! It's His building, His people, and His plans that unfolded in our midst. The gentleman who closed the purchase of the property said in 35 years of the business, he had never seen a transaction like ours. We were even given 100,000 dollars cash from the seller toward the purchase of their building. The banker was absolutely dumbfounded.

I want to encourage all pioneers who are discouraged, weary, and tired to keep believing God for the impossible! Whether you feel called to plant a house church or assemble in a large building, do not get distracted on the structure but rather focus your attention on the DNA God is calling you to establish. Do not waste your time fighting or comparing with others the type of wineskin God has called you to build. It's all about the new wine! You might not need to attend another conference, seminar, or leadership training to be obedient to what God has called you to do. Get into the place of prayer and fasting and watch the heavens come down in your midst.

If God has not told you to join a denomination, then don't! If God has not told you to join a network, then don't! Networking and connecting with people who have larger platforms and influence is oftentimes not the answer to what you need. I'm convinced through experience that much of the current "church planting" models and "networks" and advice being given to many pioneers and church planters cannot be found in the New Testament. Your job is not to be some CEO of a new church plant or join the next greatest and latest network; your calling is down on your face being the servant of all. Rear ends in seats, how many services you are running, and dollars in the offering doesn't define you or how successful you are. May the Holy Spirit bring great strength, supernatural vision, and encouragement to church planters and pioneers from around the world today. Keep your eyes on Jesus. He loves you and is cheering you on!

At twenty years old, I could have never imagined what would unfold in the months and years ahead. On that floor at the conference where I wept in agony, begging God to please not ask me to plant a church, was a young man who knew the very thing I feared was the very thing God was calling me to do. Though the cost was great and God truly blessed us, one of the things I was not prepared for was the jealousy and attacks that would come in the years that followed from fellow church leaders and family members. As a pioneer and trailblazer, you will not only pay a price for the work that you are actively establishing, but there will also be a cost exacted in your friendships and relationships.

THE ATTACKS ON PIONEERS

"As a pioneer, you cannot do the will of God without challenging the way things have always been and causing catalytic changes in the Body of Christ." This will inevitably cause many to stumble, scoff, criticize, and falsely accuse you."

There is a demonic strategy set up against every pioneer in their generation that is not only aimed at destroying them, but also scattering the followers. If satan's attack is successful, everyone involved will come out of the battle hurt and wounded. Remember, satan uses people to attack, criticize, and question pioneers so that those who are getting set free, refreshed, and empowered by their life and ministry will become confused, disoriented, and altogether stop listening to the emerging pioneers.

Pioneers, you cannot allow yourself to become so easily manipulated by people's criticisms and attacks. Do not try to maintain peace in your heart and life based off of whether people accept or reject you. From my own personal experiences, most of the time God will not deliver you from your accusers, but rather He will actually save you by killing the part of you that is vulnerable to the devil by using the accusations themselves.

As a pioneer, you must recognize that both God and the devil want you to die, but for different reasons. Satan wants to destroy you through attacks and criticisms and then drain you by your unwavering need to explain yourself and your side of the story. (Please stop wasting your time and energy doing this!) On the other hand, God wants to crucify that part in you that was so easily exploited by the devil to begin with. "The rest and peace that you are so desiring in your life and ministry will only come when you finally die to what people say and think about you."

Pioneers, in order to deliver you from the praise of men, God will baptize you in their criticisms and attacks. It is painful. You will lose many friendships along the way and the misunderstandings will be many. You will pay a price that most around you will never see nor understand. You are speaking a language of reform and awakening that many in the Body of Christ just don't have an eye or ear for yet. Do not grow discouraged and, most of all, do not be surprised when the attacks and criticisms come. Rather than rushing to defend or explain yourself, my advice would be to go before the Lord and ask Him, "What inside of me are You exposing through the accusation and attacks of others that needs to die?"

I admit as an emerging pioneer in this generation that I have not always responded well to the attacks and criticisms of many. The loss of friendships and the misunderstandings have been very painful over the years. I was truly unprepared for what lay ahead of me when God began to open major doors in the Body of Christ some years ago on a national level. My sincere hope and prayer is that my mistakes and ultimately the revelation of what I have shared above might benefit other pioneers. Your perspective and response to the attacks and criticisms of others will define and shape you far more than you will ever realize. I'm eternally grateful for several spiritual fathers who have walked me through these pioneering years, and I apologize to those whom I might have unnecessarily offended along my journey pursuing the mandate God has given me. Who knew that God is so good that He chooses to use even the accusations and attacks of our enemies to conform us into the image and likeness of Jesus Christ. May God grant us His grace to remain broken, humbled, and ultimately delivered from both the praise and criticism of men.

A PROPHETIC WORD TO PIONEERS

Killing Goliath was both the *best* and *worst* event that ever happened to young David! (See First Samuel 17.) Be warned, emerging pioneers—that big open door, that promotion, that spotlight, that book signing, that revival, that television interview you know you were born for will unleash the greatest jealousy, insecurity, and slander from fathers/mothers and brothers/sisters that you have ever known, but will also set the stage for you to fulfill your destiny in the earth. A generation of fathers (Saul) could only celebrate David so long as he would wear his armor. Once David became more successful than Saul by killing Goliath and defeating the Philistines, his jealousy would hunt David the rest of his life.

Be warned, emerging pioneers—some of those fathers/mothers who once cheered you on in your earlier years when you were in their shadow will despise you, slander you, and try to kill your influence as you surpass them in anointing and grace. Their words will sting you, try to poison and confuse you, and derail you from pursuing God with all your might! A generation of peers (Eliab and Abinadab) could only see David as their baby brother and the insignificant one who tended to the little sheep. Once David knew he was ready to cut the head off Goliath and he did, the jealousy and insecurity of David's brothers soared!

Be warned, emerging pioneers—some of those brothers/sisters you once ran with and were even constantly overlooked with because of their talents and skills will writhe in anger, jealousy, and insecurity as they watch you fulfill your destiny. They will stir up gossip, slander, and false accusations among brothers/sisters around your own age simply because they cannot stand that God chose you to fulfill this assignment and not them!

To the emerging pioneers, I say—keep praying, keep dreaming, and keep pressing, but do not disregard this prophetic warning of the days that lie ahead of you! Count the cost. Recognize the spiritual warfare that is about to be unleashed against you and yours. You will lose some good fathers and mothers who once encouraged you as a rookie and will not be able to stand you as an emerging pioneer. Pray for them and honor them the best you know how. They just can't see you the way God sees you. Don't become distracted or disappointed with the Eliabs and Abinadabs (brothers and sisters) around you. They once ran with you and spoke well of you and now their insecurity will cause them to want to see your downfall. When they spread rumors about you, choose to speak good of them. God will bless you.

Finally, emerging pioneers, be warned, but also be encouraged! Your Jonathans are coming to your rescue! You maybe once had fathers/mothers who no longer pour into you and maybe even brothers/sisters whom you were once close with and no longer talk with, but a company of Jonathans quickly comes to your side! They will get you and the assignment on your life. They will celebrate what God has put in you and called you to do. They are willing to run with you, but really they just want to be your friend! They will defend you to the death to the Sauls and whispering voices all around you. As you emerge, grow in your calling, and navigate the wilderness, they will be with you every step of the way. The days ahead will be great for you emerging pioneers, but they will also be full of testing and trials. Keep your eyes on Jesus and you will run your race!

THE POWER OF ACCOUNTABLE RELATIONSHIPS

Pioneering can be a very lonely journey. It is oftentimes filled with rejection, disappointment, and heartache. One of the primary ways I have learned to keep my heart clean before the Lord is understanding and embracing the power of true fathering. Not every church, ministry, or leader is out to get you. In fact, if pioneers are not careful to guard their hearts from bitterness and resentment, they will end up rejecting the very individuals God has sent to help them.

I believe it is so important for pioneers to walk in true accountable relationships with fathers that the devil will do everything he can to try to sabotage that process. In early 2015, I stood on a stage with thousands of people in attendance at a national conference in the United States. I preached a message on our most urgent national need—for God to raise up true prophets in the land.

As corporate intercession and travail broke out in the masses, weeping hit me so hard that I fell to my knees in the middle of the message and cried out, "The prophets in America have dined at Jezebel's table for too long and a new breed of Micaiahs is coming forth." As the intensity of the intercession and travail picked up, suddenly a father in the nation came to the stage and took the microphone and asked me to sit down. He did it graciously, but proceeded to shut down the meeting and spent the next 30 minutes apologizing for what just happened. I sat in the front row with tears in my eyes. I was embarrassed, stunned, and incredibly shamed in front of so many people.

In the back room after the service, the national father in the faith told me I was just too intense, too zealous, and the intercession and travail that took place was too much to steward at the conference. I left that weekend totally stabbed to my core. I spent the next six months in professional counseling, fasting, and considering shutting down my travel ministry. Because I considered this man a spiritual father and forerunner, the wounds and insecurity it created in me ran deep—real deep!

By God's sovereign grace, I was able to forgive after a period of deep inner healing, and some personal soul-searching, to take any responsibility for what I might have done wrong as a son. It wasn't until 2018 that I found myself speaking at yet another national conference with thousands of people, and the father who had wounded me so deeply in 2015 was also a speaker! The day he flew in for the conference, I received a text from him (we had not spoken in almost three years). He asked to meet with me. To my great surprise and astonishment, he got down on his knees with tears and repented to me at the meeting. I was stunned! But it brought yet another wave of healing and forgiveness over my soul.

Through my own tears and sobs, I heard the voice of God speak so clearly that day. He said, "Jeremiah, the devil intended to rob you of your inheritance as a son to many fathers in this nation, but his strategy has been thwarted today as a more excellent way has been established. The path of forgiveness and love has delivered you from the cancer of bitterness and resentment. I have called you to minister to the sons and daughters who have been wounded by the fathers. Great bitterness has filled their souls and will become poison to their destinies."

If God is speaking to your heart right now, I encourage you to put down this book for a moment and do some serious soul-searching. Are you wounded and bitter toward the Church or a leader in the Body of Christ? Is a spirit of rejection operating in your life to the point where you do not trust any type of authority? I encourage you to write a letter to that church leader who hurt you and release them to God. Send a financial offering to someone who has hurt you on your spiritual journey and watch God promote you to new levels in His Sprit. Like David, let us pray this powerful prayer together as we pioneer the way forward into this new era: *"Search me, O God, and know my heart: try me, and know my thoughts: and see if there be any wicked way in me, and lead me in the way everlasting"* (Ps. 139:23-24, KJV).

Chapter 3

THE DECREE
FROM HEAVEN

As I mentioned in the last chapter, I planted a church called "Heart of the Father Ministry" in Lakeland, Florida in 2010. At the time, I was very confident in the future of the church and the vision I was carrying. I had attended a four-year Bible college and received a bachelor's degree, grew up immersed in the things of God, and now I was ready to build a house of glory around the gifts and calling God had given me. I had every intention of planting a one-man ministry!

As I laid down to sleep one night early in this pioneering journey, I quickly realized that not only was I mistaken about what I thought God called me to do (and most of what I learned in Bible college), but I was in store for the greatest wakeup call of my life—an encounter with God that has marked me forever!

THE PROPHETIC DREAM

That night in a dream, I found myself in one of the most profound prophetic experiences of my life. I was standing in front of a door that was as tall as my eyes could see. To the left and right of the door was brick stone. I immediately noticed that there was an inscription in the brick to the right of the door that read, "Good shepherds do not treat people like sheep. Shepherds are sheep also, and they need to lead people in the same manner as they themselves are led by the Lord." After I read the inscription aloud in amazement, the large door in front of me opened and I walked into the most beautiful, lively, colorful, and vast place I have ever visited or seen in my life.

"Extravagant" does not do it justice! Inside this place were celestial and angelic beings. Some were the size of an average human, and others were extremely large. Many of them had beautifully colored wings and some glowed so bright that I couldn't help but gaze upon the beauty of their splendor. I saw colors and heard sounds that I had previously never encountered or seen to this day. As I began to make my way forward, I realized that

I was in no ordinary place. I said out loud in the dream, "This is none other than the heavenly courts!"

As those words left my lips, suddenly, three golden thrones appeared in the distance before me. There was one throne for the Holy Spirit, one for Jesus, and one for the Father. Holy fear began to grip my heart as I locked eyes with the Lord Jesus Christ for the very first time in my life. He was sitting at the right hand of the Father. I began to tremble at the beauty and majesty that was seated before me.

I began to fix my eyes upon the golden throne in the center where the Father was, yet I could not make out His figure. I only knew by the glory and presence I felt that He was there. I took several steps to try to close the distance between me and the golden thrones, and instantly seven angels stood at my left and my right. I stood there stunned, gazing into their faces that radiated joy and delight. They smiled at me and looked toward the Father's throne, as did I.

A holy hush fell within the heavenly courts and I heard God the Father's voice. He began to speak to me saying, "The seven angels that stand before Me with you are the angels of the seven churches. The seven churches represent my corporate body." He paused and then said, "I summon you: son of man, apostles, prophets, evangelists, shepherds, and teachers—LET MY PEOPLE GO!" As He said, "Let My people go," the courts of Heaven shook and His voice thundered. My entire body stiffened and I immediately sensed in the dream that this mandate must precede the second coming of the Lord Jesus. Then I immediately awoke.

DIVINE CONVERSATION

I sat up in my bed that morning, out of breath and profusely sweating. Deeply afraid and sensing the weight of what I had just experienced, I cried out to the Lord and said, "Father, no! There is no way that you are calling me to apostles, prophets, evangelists, shepherds, and teachers in the earth with a message to let Your people go!" There was no response, only deafening silence and my mind spinning wildly.

I began to tremble even thinking of telling people that I actually went to Heaven. "They are going to label me a false prophet!" I spoke aloud in the silence of my room. I then said to God, "Father, what are Your people not doing that You want them to do?" His voice spoke clearly to me and said, "Jeremiah, why did I free My people from Egypt?" I said, "Because You had called them to the Promised Land." He said, "Wrong answer. Go back and study the Book of Exodus and I will meet you there."

I quickly jumped out of my bed and opened my Bible. I read the entire Book of Exodus in one sitting that morning, and there the answer was before my eyes, time and time again.

- Exodus 7:16: "Let My people go, that they may *serve Me* in the wilderness."
- Exodus 8:1: "Let My people go, that they may *serve Me.*"
- Exodus 9:1: "Let My people go, that they may *serve Me.*"
- Exodus 9:13: "Let My people go, that they may *serve Me.*"
- Exodus 10:3: "Let My people go, that they may *serve Me.*"

After finishing the Book of Exodus, I found myself arguing with the Lord that day and for many weeks after that. "What are You talking about, God? Your people are serving You." Then His words would pierce my heart like an arrow for months on end:

> *Jeremiah, My people are not serving Me, nor are they worshiping Me in a way that is pleasing to Me, for they have become more comfortable serving men, serving their ministries, and worshiping at their feet than they are serving, ministering to, and worshiping Me.*

As He would further share His heart concerning these matters, I would experience seasons of great weeping and travail. As I cried out for greater wisdom and revelation concerning this dream, one day He said to me:

> *Jeremiah, the current wineskin of church leadership in the earth cannot contain the new wine that I am about to pour out in My Church. You must tell church leadership to let My people go. They must not accept the worship of the people any longer. I am about to shake the very foundation of the Church. In the years to come, you will see a new apostolic generation rise who will build according to the pattern that I have set forth in Scripture. They will expose the kingdoms of Sauls, who are building their own names and ministries, and call forth fivefold ministry leaders with a Davidic anointing who will walk humbly before Me. If my apostles, prophets, evangelists, shepherds, and teachers will listen to My voice and let the people go, I will reward them with levels of glory that have never been seen before upon the earth. If they refuse, three judgments will fall upon them—family crisis, personal burnout, and moral failure.*

I must admit that since the night of that prophetic dream, and then conversations with the Lord over the following months, my life has never been the same. I was about to make one of the biggest mistakes of my life by building a one-man ministry centered around my gifts and calling, but the grace of God spared me! I'm so grateful, but still to this day I have been shaken to my core, and the truth is I am still feeling the weight of what I was shown even up to this very hour. I have only shared the prophetic dream and experience you just read on several public occasions. Why? It has been too much of a fearful and weighty encounter just to share flippantly. In Chapter 1, I specifically mentioned the word God spoke to me while I was preaching during the COVID-19 pandemic. He said:

> *Oh, how My heart breaks for the lost sheep who are not being taught how to feed on My word and worship Me. Rather, they are being falsely deceived into man worship, which is idolatry. Repent of celebrity Christianity and recognize the window of time I have now opened for a divine reset in the global Church.*

Could one of the primary hindrances to God filling His house with glory in the new era be the celebrity Christianity we worship in America and other nations? Is there too much emphasis on the gifting and charisma of men and not enough adoration and awe focused on the person of Jesus Christ? The answers to these valid questions and more are ahead in the next chapter as we enter the new era together!

Chapter 4
_____

THE FIVEFOLD MINISTRY

"*J*eremiah, the new wine that I am about to pour out upon My Bride cannot be contained in the existing one-man ministry structure upon which the Church has been built." This was the revelation the Father gave me concerning His mandate to church leadership to "Let My people go" in Chapter 3. As I have prayed deeper into the encounter, God spoke to me again:

> *For years, contemporary church leadership has tried to model everything in the Book of Acts and the Epistles except the governmental structure that I set in place. Too many are chasing the miracles, the community, and the outpouring of My Spirit, but they will never taste of the new wine I*

> *desire to send to My Bride unless they learn how*
> *to build My house of glory according to My heart*
> *and pattern as found in the Scriptures.*

DIFFICULT QUESTIONS

As I began to seek God and examine the Scriptures to find the "pattern" He desired, I was stunned at my findings. I was searching for examples in the New Testament where one gifted individual was called to have complete authority and leadership over a body of believers. I couldn't find any. I was in shock and began asking difficult questions. What if the greatest hindrance to a next Great Awakening is not the sin of the world or even the Church? "What if the greatest obstacle to a genuine move of God is the way our current church leadership models are structured?"

THE EXAMPLE OF JESUS

As I began to reexamine and take a deeper look into the ministry of Jesus Christ, it became very clear to me that forming a team was a top priority for Him, even though He came from heaven and was sent by the Father. He was obviously graced with all authority and vision, yet recognized the power of having a team of leaders around Him. Did Jesus flippantly choose men who would become apostles and eventually pioneer the first-century Church? No, His choices were actually so important that, before choosing them, He spent the whole night in prayer (see Luke 6:12-13). If this is the example of Jesus Christ, the greatest apostle and pioneer (see Heb. 3:1), how have we managed to gather saints in buildings where one gifted individual is the only one who can preach and lead?

By gathering a team of leaders around Himself, Jesus wanted to establish both a *relational* base that would be a prototype for future pioneers and apostolic ministries, and a *functional* unit capable of carrying out the mandate to establish the Kingdom here on earth. *"And He appointed twelve, so that they would be with Him* [relational base] *and that He could send them out to preach, and to have authority to cast out the demons* [functional capacity*]"* (Mark 3:14-15).

THE EXAMPLE OF PAUL

Barnabas was perhaps the first individual to recognize the grace on Paul's life. He went to Tarsus to look for him and brought him to Antioch. There they taught in the church for an entire year. From that house of glory, the Holy Spirit set apart and commissioned Paul and Barnabas to plant more houses of glory throughout the Mediterranean world. Please take note that one gifted individual like Paul did not travel alone, but rather always functioned alongside another leader.

Paul only knew the Holy Spirit was sending him to preach with Barnabas, but they ended up establishing communities of believers and appointing elders everywhere they went. They would then return to report to Antioch, their sending base. This is a tremendous example of accountability and a desire for community among the early apostles. Unfortunately, there is a serious lack of team ministry and relational accountability among many apostles and pioneers today. I will seek to address this issue in the final chapter of this book.

After reporting back to Antioch, Paul took another trip to see how the saints were maturing in Christ, this time with Silas, a prophet (see Acts 15:32). It would only be a short time until Paul added Timothy to this team (see Acts 16:1-3). Although called as an apostle to plant churches, Paul was constantly surrounding himself with other fivefold ministers. He recognized the need for the grace of Jesus Christ to be fully present and active on his team.

THE MINISTRY OF JESUS AND PAUL

Jesus Christ came first as the Chief Apostle, commissioned twelve apostles whom He directly walked with, and then later commissioned Paul and countless other pioneers in the years ahead to establish His Kingdom and plant churches. However, there was always grace to establish teams around them. By Paul's third missionary journey, there were entire teams mobilized and traveling with him to spread the Gospel (see Acts 20:4-6). In Mark 6:7, Jesus lays hands on the apostles and sends them out two by two to proclaim and demonstrate the Kingdom. In order to build houses of glory in the earth that can hold the new wine God so desires to pour out, we must confront the unbiblical paradigms functioning in way too many churches where one gifted individual is tasked with doing all the leading and public ministry.

THE PLANTING OF CHURCHES

As apostles like Paul, Barnabas, Timothy, and Titus began winning souls for Christ in various cities, planting churches, establishing Jesus Christ as the foundation of the Church, and discipling new believers, they eventually laid hands on elder teams and commissioned them to shepherd, teach, lead, protect, and oversee the saints in each city where disciples became churches. Here are some biblical examples:

- Elders governed the church in Jerusalem (Acts 15).

- Elders are found in the churches of Judea and the surrounding area (Acts 11:30; James 5:14-15).

- Elders were established in the churches of Derbe, Lystra, Iconium, and Antioch (Acts 14:23); in the church at Ephesus (Acts 20:17; 1 Tim. 3:1-7; 5:17-25); in the church at Philippi (Phil. 1:1); and in the churches on the island of Crete (Titus 1:5).

- According to Peter, a plurality of elders existed in churches throughout northwestern Asia minor—Pontus, Galatia, Cappadocia, Asia, and Bithynia (1 Pet. 1:1; 5:1).

Did you know that the New Testament offers more instruction regarding elders in the church than baptism, spiritual gifts, and the Lord's Supper? Again, many search for why we are falling so short of what we read in the Book of Acts and the Epistles, and I'm sounding the alarm—the way we have chosen to build houses of glory is our main limitation and hindrance to training and equipping the saints, which will usher in the greatest revival and subsequent reformation we have ever known. The global Body of Christ is not being trained and equipped to reach the fullness of the knowledge of the Son of God because they are only being exposed to the ministry of one man on a consistent basis.

When COVID-19 effectively shut down almost every corporate gathering of believers in America and every nation of the earth, had there been enough training and equipping of the saints done so that houses of glory could thrive during global shaking? On the contrary, what we discovered statistically by Barna and other research groups is that large portions of the Church crumbled and grew lethargic, all due to the fact that the saints could no longer rely on one man or woman to teach them the Word of God. As we enter into the new era, we are going to see an explosion of various training and equipping centers all over the earth that will seek to address this serious and painful truth that was uncovered by the coronavirus. Houses of glory are going to emerge in neighborhoods, inner cities, coffee shops, and anywhere groups of people can gather. There will be much more of a necessary emphasis on shared leadership and the priesthood of all believers than there ever was prior to COVID-19.

Let's take a look at instructions that were given to the *elders,* not single leaders, in the New Testament:

- James instructs those who are sick to call upon the *elders* of the church (James 5:14).

- Paul instructs the Ephesian church to financially support *elders* who labor at "preaching and teaching" (1 Tim. 5:17-18).

- Paul instructs the church as to proper qualifications for *eldership* (1 Tim. 3:1-7; Tit. 1:5-9). When Paul lays out the qualifications for elders, he clearly envisions each qualified individual to be a part of a team, not the single leader of any congregation.

- Peter instructs the young men to submit to the church *elders* (1 Pet. 5:5).

- The writer of Hebrews instructs his readers to obey and submit to the *leaders* (Heb. 13:17).

- Paul instructs the church to acknowledge, love, and live at peace with its *leaders* (1 Thess. 5:12-13).

In his *Systematic Theology*, Wayne Grudem says:

No passage in the New Testament suggests that any church, no matter how small, had only one senior leader. The consistent New Testament pattern is a plurality of elders "in every church" (Acts 14:23) and "in every town" (Titus 1:5). We do not see a diversity of forms of government in the New Testament church, but a unified and consistent pattern in which every church had elders governing it and keeping watch over it (Acts 20:28; Heb. 13:17; 1 Peter 5:2-3).[1]

How can there be so many references to multiple elders giving oversight and leadership to the local church in the New Testament, yet this structure of church leadership can hardly be found in America and many parts of the world? How have we strayed so far from what was considered the normal way of appointing leaders to govern houses of glory in the New Testament? Once again, could it be true that the greatest resistance to new wine being poured out upon this generation is celebrity Christianity that seeks to exalt the one-man ministries we have built? Could God also be exposing supposed team ministries that are really one-man ministries because they operate as a pyramidal hierarchy? Are we asking God to fill a church model He never formed and created to begin with? Isaiah rightly prophesies, *"The new wine is found in the cluster* [team]" (Isa. 65:8).

ELDERS AND THE FIVEFOLD MINISTRY

From what we have just read in the New Testament, the pattern revealed to us is one in which apostles are called to establish churches where they are responsible for revealing the mysteries of Christ, discipling new converts, and then eventually laying hands on a plurality of elders who are given charge to shepherd the flock together. Having multiple elders governing a body of believers, as opposed to one man, not only protects the headship of Jesus Christ so that only He may receive preeminence, but it also allows for multiple fivefold graces to function in a house of glory. Bible scholar Wayne Grudem says:

> A practical problem with a "single man" system is either an excessive concentration of power in one person or excessive demands laid upon him. In either case, the temptations to sin are very great. It was never the pattern in the New Testament, even with the apostles, to concentrate ruling power in the hands of any one person.[2]

As apostles plant churches and eventually establish eldership teams who have a fivefold ministry call on their lives, a training and equipping of the saints is allowed to take place that is simply impossible with a one-man ministry running the show. As exemplified by Paul, the apostle who planted the church typically moves on to plant another one after he has laid Jesus Christ as the foundation, cornerstone, and head of His Church and established a plurality of elders to govern the affairs of the church. If the apostle who planted the church chooses to remain at the church that he planted among the eldership team, he becomes a fellow elder who functions apostolically in their midst, but he cannot usurp the elders or be domineering over them. He must choose to come alongside of them so that the fivefold ministry might be fully expressed in the body of believers (see 1 Pet. 5:1).

If the founding apostle plants the church and after some time decides to move on geographically to plant and establish other churches and ministries, the elder-ship team, previously approved by the apostle, should continue to walk in relationship with the apostle for mutual accountability and relationship among the team members. This will allow for the fivefold ministry to continue to operate both locally and abroad.

APOSTLES AND ELDERS

God is looking for partnership and mutual submis-sion between apostles and elders. Both must honor one another and demonstrate the proper attitudes of humility and respect. Elders are not children. They are qualified individuals with grace and gifting to lead. Thus, apostles should never treat them this way, but rather as fellow workers. The end goal should be as though the apostle(s) and elders make major decisions together (an example of which can be seen practically in Acts 15:6-7, 23).

Once proper foundation has been laid and the apostle lays hands on the elders, the apostle should not try to micromanage the local church. This is the call and mandate of the local elders who are on the ground (see 1 Tim. 5:17). In certain areas, the apostle should be granted the liberty to speak, but they must not get overly involved if at all possible. The primary calling of apostles is to enlarge the Kingdom, not to micromanage it. While apostles expand the Kingdom and seek to keep it healthy, local church elders are entrusted with the day-to-day management of it. Apostles come as servants of the church, not as masters of it (see 1 Cor. 3:5; 4:1; 2 Cor. 4:5; 6:4; 11:23). The simple truth here is this—apostolic authority is never demanded; it is recognized.

DIVINE TENSION

It's critical that you understand that I am not communicating mere theory. I had the privilege for ten years to plant a church, cast vision and give leadership, build deep relationships in a community of believers, and function as an elder on a team of other fivefold ministers. When God called me to move geographically to establish other ministries, I laid hands on the elders and commissioned them to continue the work of the Lord. To this day, Heart of the Father Ministry is an established work in Lakeland, Florida serving the purposes of God in our generation. Along our journey toward healthy fivefold ministry, I also laid hands on a second elder team and commissioned them with a tremendous group of saints to establish a second campus in Winter Haven, Florida. For almost the first two years of this new church plant, I committed to help serve, preach, and give oversight to the eldership team as they pioneered the Kingdom of God in a new region. I have not only been a personal witness to the glory, struggles, and balance that the fivefold ministries bring, but I have also had the privilege of overseeing and establishing other churches and ministries around the world.

As a former elder on a leadership team with different fivefold ministry callings, I understand the divine tension that can exist because of the grace on each leader's life. If you sat an apostle, prophet, evangelist, shepherd, and teacher down and asked them what God was saying to His Church, each of them would give you a different answer because of the unique grace on their lives. The apostle would say the Church needs more biblical identity, fathering, discipleship, body relationships, qualified elders, order, and power. The prophet would say the Church needs more holiness, spiritual maturity, relevance in the public square, and growth in the Spirit's gifts. The evangelist would say people are dying and going to hell! We need to preach the Gospel, get people saved, and we feed the poor. The shepherd would say that people are hurting and broken and need healing, wisdom, protection, and counsel from the Word and Spirit. The teacher would say that the Church needs to learn the Word of God more for discipleship, accurate doctrine, balance, and maturity. What a beautiful thing it is to have different ministries carrying five different portions of who Jesus Christ is, yet called to work together in unity! It is a beautiful thing when apostles, prophets, evangelists, shepherds, and teachers work together in one community of believers! "Functioning together as a team of fivefold ministers does not minimize one another's gifting, but actually maximizes them!"

The vision and direction of each church plant should be primarily governed in the early stages by the apostle who planted the work. However, when the elder team is eventually commissioned to lead in a greater capacity and the apostle begins to travel and carries a God-given burden for other regions and nations, the vision and mission of the church plant will be greatly impacted by what fivefold ministry calling the elders have. In other words, each local church expression is going to have a certain flavor because of the shared leadership of the eldership team. For example, we know in the church of Antioch there were several prophets and teachers, a combination that would have given that church a unique mandate as a body of believers (see Acts 13:1).

It's important during transitional seasons of leadership that relationships are guarded from the attacks of the enemy. The vision that apostles and prophets carry from the Spirit of God is directed toward the wider Body of Christ. This is in contrast to shepherds and teachers who carry vision from the Holy Spirit that is generally directed toward a specific and local gathering of people. Without the vision that apostles and prophets carry, local churches become self-focused, stagnant, and are constantly plagued by tunnel vision. These assemblies primarily become inward focused over time rather than empowered to advance the Kingdom in their city and region.

If you are a shepherd or teacher and do not acknowledge and invite the ministries of the apostles and prophets into your church community, the vision you have there is too small and must be expanded. You must invite the prophets (they see) and the apostles (they mobilize) to impart a greater vision and plan of action in your midst. It takes a heart of humility to confess that we as church leaders need one another. The fivefold ministry must learn how to work together in this hour!

FURTHER CLARIFICATION

As I have interacted with so many church leaders around the world over the last ten years and shared what you have just read, many of them believe they are already doing what I am explaining. These ministers who respond like this are typically the senior pastor of their church and they have a paid or volunteer staff who do whatever they say. But this scenario is the farthest example from what I am talking about.

On the contrary, when the fivefold ministry is fully operational in a community of believers, it will primarily have an impact in public settings and community gatherings. At Heart of the Father Ministry, our leadership team shared the church's pastoral responsibilities, including a weekly preaching rotation, counseling appointments, discipleship, and caring for the flock. Over the years, many visitors were stunned to visit our church and find out that as a national and international conference speaker, I was not speaking at the church that Sunday or Wednesday. I was actually receiving the Word from one of our elders and spending time with my family. For many years our leadership team also met weekly to pray together, fast as needed, and build deep love and relationship with one another. The truth is that jealousy, insecurity, and pride will not survive doing team ministry together. I love what Alexander Strauch writes and says concerning team leadership in the local church:

> Establishing healthy biblical eldership requires the elders to show mutual regard and concern for one another, submit themselves to one another, patiently wait upon one another, and defer and prefer one another. Eldership thus enhances brotherly love, humility, and mutuality. Learning how to lead and care for the flock together will expose impatience with one another, stubbornness, bull-headedness, selfish-immaturity, domineering dispositions, prayerlessness, pride, and jealousy.[3]

APOSTOLIC GRACE

Each of the five ministries that the Lord has given to His Church in Ephesians 4:11 (apostles, prophets, evangelists, shepherds, and teachers) has a specific grace that determines their function. For example, Paul says that the foundation of the Church is built upon the apostles and prophets (see Eph. 2:20). In other words, the two ministries of apostles and prophets carry unique grace to lay the foundation of God's house that evangelists, shepherds, and teachers cannot lay. That is not the grace God has given them. While apostles and prophets are foundation layers, evangelists, shepherds, and teachers have building ministries. Where in the New Testament do you ever find a pastor or evangelist planting a church?

One of the primary issues in the global Church is that we have attempted to establish houses of glory with only teachers, shepherds, and evangelists (building ministries) without the foundational ministries of apostles and prophets. Reaping what we have sown, we now have a global Church that in many places is a mile wide and an inch deep. It looks beautiful on the outside, but the foundation is crumbling because of the way we have chosen to build. When Jesus Christ returns, will He say to us "Well done!" or "What have you done?"

FOUNDATION LAYERS

Please do not misunderstand what I am saying. Apostles and prophets are not better than evangelists, shepherds, and teachers. This is not a competition, nor is it a hierarchy. We are discussing the sequence for properly building the wineskin that will hold the new wine God wants to pour out in every generation. This is about recognizing the grace on certain ministries and allowing them to function according to the scriptural pattern. Not every individual who graduates from Bible college or seminary is a "pastor." Not every person who enters into ministry is a "teacher." "What happens if he is called by God and given grace to be an "apostle" or "prophet"? Our religious denominations do not have room, or even a paradigm, for such biblical foundations!"

Paul says, *"And God has appointed in the church, first apostles, second prophets, third teachers, then miracles, then gifts of healings, helps, administrations, various kinds of tongues"* (1 Cor. 12:28). Why has God first appointed apostles and then prophets in the Church? Because they alone carry the grace and blueprints to lay a proper foundation for the Church. What exactly is that grace? Listen to what else Paul says about this very point:

According to the grace of God which was given to me, like a wise master builder I laid a foundation, and another is building on it. But each man must be careful how he builds on it. For no man can lay a foundation other than the one which is laid, which is Jesus Christ (1 Corinthians 3:10-11).

APOSTLES REVEAL JESUS CHRIST

Apostolic grace was given to Paul to uncover and unveil the true foundation of the Church, Jesus Christ. Apostles carry specific and unique grace to reveal the person of Jesus to His body. Apostolic preaching is the preaching of Christ and Him crucified (see 1 Cor. 2:1-2). If we cancel and negate the ministry of apostles in the Body of Christ, then we are removing the very individuals who carry the grace to connect us to our true head, source, foundation, and cornerstone—Jesus Christ! I recently read an article by a well-known "apostle" in the Body of Christ who listed fifteen functions of apostles. There was not a single mention of revealing Jesus Christ to His body in the list. How far our modern-day apostolic ministry has fallen from the example and blueprint Paul left us in Scripture! Paul goes on to say:

Now if any man builds on the foundation with gold, silver, precious stones, wood, hay, straw, each man's work will become evident; for the day will show it because it is to be revealed with fire, and the fire itself will test the quality of each man's work (1 Corinthians 3:12-13).

There is a tangible fire that is going to come and test the global Church. How we have chosen to build the house of God will be exposed. Where there are no apostles and apostolic grace functioning, Jesus Christ is not being revealed for who He really is. It is also noteworthy that earlier in this same chapter, Paul addresses the tendency for apostolic ministry to attract a cult following. Not only do we need apostolic order to return to the Church so Jesus might take preeminence in all things, but we also need so-called "apostles" who are building their own kingdoms to repent and step aside. The problem with much of our contemporary apostolic ministry is that it brings a takeover mentality to the Church where supposed apostles build cult-like followings after themselves. They operate in a Diotrephes spirit and want first place in all things (see 3 John 1:9). This is a tremendous tragedy because true apostles are the very ones who carry the grace to connect the body to our true head,

Jesus Christ. Remember, Paul never created a cult following at Corinth but rather rejected and condemned it. Any true modern-day apostle would do the same!

Most people fail to recognize that apostolic ministry refuses to build upon any other foundation than Jesus Christ (see 1 Cor. 3:10; Eph. 2:20). True apostles will tear down any foundation besides Jesus Christ in God's house. If a ministry or church has been built upon someone's gifting, personality, or charisma, a true apostle will call it out and tear it down. If a ministry or church has been built by pastors and teachers without that foundational revelation of Jesus Christ, a true apostle will expose the faulty foundations and seek to establish apostolic order within that body. Many church leaders want to invite the ministry of apostles in their midst. But if that church is not founded on Jesus, there is going to be a tremendous amount of apostolic order that will need to be established to replace the old order.

APOSTLES DO MORE THAN
PLANT CHURCHES

A large portion of apostolic grace is the setting of things into proper order and function (see 1 Cor. 11:34; Col. 2:5; Tit. 1:5). For example, apostles establish the doctrines of Christ, father spiritual children, correct problems, ordain elders, uproot and tear down false doctrines, and challenge false teachers. This mandate requires great time and effort on their part in one community of believers.

Apostles are wise master builders (see 1 Cor. 3:10). In other words, when they detect that a proper foundation has not been laid (Jesus Christ as the cornerstone and foundation), they will overthrow, uproot, tear down, and destroy before they begin to build and bring multiplication. It is for this reason that perhaps true apostles are not invited into many existing church structures because of the evident grace upon their lives.

Rather than having a couple of "revival services" over a weekend, true apostles will inquire and ask the hard questions to eldership teams. They will not blow in and out over a weekend for a quick honorarium. Apostles carry a tremendous father's heart that is concerned for the welfare of those they are called to serve. The truth be told, apostolic work is extremely difficult and oftentimes takes years in one location! Paul did not spend a weekend in Ephesus. He spent three years there (see Acts 20:31) and a year and a half in Corinth (see Acts 18:11). In other cities and regions, he spent as much time as needed, or as much as he was physically able. Calling people "apostles" who blow in and out of cities and have no hand in actually building and establishing houses of glory on a consistent basis is absurd! Even worse, there are so-called "apostles" floating around the earth right now claiming apostolic grace, but they have never planted a church, laid hands on eldership teams, nor fathered the fivefold ministry.

I see God raising up apostles who are sound in the doctrines of Christ, who carry a specific anointing to set a body of believers into proper order and function, and who are radically committed to spending lengthy amounts of time and care for those God has called them to serve. The foundation and revelation of Jesus Christ must return to the global Church in this hour. And that cannot come without authentic apostles.

SEVEN ASSIGNMENTS OF APOSTLES

The New Testament reveals seven specific assignments entrusted to apostles as they function among a body of believers.

1. *They exercise discipline.*

According to the New Testament, apostles were involved in the disciplining and discipling of elders. Apostles work with eldership teams to ensure the individuals leading are living a life above reproach.

Character and integrity are always prioritized above gifting in the New Testament. Apostles are also graced in helping elder teams grow in their leadership abilities and challenging them concerning their time in the Word and prayer (see Tit. 1:5-9; 1 Tim. 3:1-7).

2. *They release sound doctrine and confront false doctrine.*

As foundation layers, apostles are graced with a revelation of Christ Jesus and the mysteries of God's Kingdom. They give special attention to detail concerning the faith that believers are called to walk in. They are also guardians against false doctrine and will at times call out false teachers and specific sin among God's people and leaders (see 1 Tim. 6:3-5; 2 Cor. 11:13-15).

3. *They strengthen the Church.*

Apostles strengthen the church by imparting spiritual gifts to the people (see Rom. 1:11). When apostles are working in a local church, there is a greater grace flowing into the church that releases the Holy Spirit and power to help establish an existing church in its biblical identity. Where apostles are functioning, elder teams are built up and the saints are stirred toward love and good deeds (see Acts 20:17-28).

4. *They provide vision.*

Apostles help to steward the mysteries of the Kingdom of God and bring a wider vision and focus to the local church. Local churches that are connected to apostles begin to attract large capacity people who are burdened for their city, region, and nation. In other words, apostolic grace attracts other fivefold ministries who carry the ability to expand God's Kingdom in a way pastoral grace never can (see Acts 16:11-15).

5. *They identify and bring unity among fivefold ministers.*

Apostles carry grace to identify, gather, and equip fivefold ministers to work and function together. When apostles are released to function in the local church, the Kingdom of God is multiplied because there is a tangible unity that surfaces among those God has called to feed and train His body. An individual claiming to be an apostle, where there are no gifted and empowered fivefold ministers around them, is walking in deception concerning their calling (see Acts 20:4; Col. 1:1-8).

6. *They invest in the elders.*

Elders should not be laboring alone—as individuals or even a local team—but should feel greatly supported and encouraged by apostles. An apostle can help to bear the burdens that elders uniquely carry, be a prayer support to them, provide fatherly wisdom concerning issues in the body of believers, and release the word of the Lord to them when necessary (see Acts 20).

7. *They provide ongoing leadership training.*

Luke shows us that apostles will continue to return to churches to provide ongoing leadership training (see Acts 20:17-38). Apostles mentor/father elders on the ground to prepare them for the future of church life. It is healthy and necessary for apostles to be invited into the churches they have either planted or are relationally connected with at least once a year.

THE HEADSHIP OF JESUS CHRIST

Why is the current, contemporary church leadership structure, where one man or woman runs the show and calls the shots, such a limitation and hindrance to the glory that God wants to send the church? Why is the Father in Heaven saying to apostles, prophets, evangelists, shepherds, and teachers, "Let My people go"?

I believe the answer is found in the fact that Jesus Christ must receive the service and worship that only He, and He alone, deserves. In the first century, no leader would dare take the position or title of sole ruler, overseer, or head of the church. Alexander Strauch puts it like this:

> We Christians today...are so accustomed to speaking of "the pastor" that we do not stop and realize that the New Testament does not. This fact is profoundly significant, and we must not permit our customary practice to shield our minds from this important truth. There is only one flock and one Pastor (John 10:16), one body and one Head (Col. 1:18), one holy priesthood and one great High Priest (Heb. 4:14), one brotherhood and one Elder Brother (Rom. 8:29), one building and one Cornerstone (1 Peter 2:5), one Mediator, one Lord. Jesus Christ is "Senior Pastor," and all others are His under shepherds (1 Peter 5:4).[4]

Jesus Christ has a serious problem with our contemporary church leadership structures because they take the worship and service off of Him and place it upon mere men. One-man ministries are often guilty of calling disciples after themselves and stealing the glory that only Jesus Christ deserves. This is why in every New Testament Church, multiple elders were set in place to oversee the people so that one man would not become essential to the church's existence or the focus of the people.

As Robert Greenleaf says in his book *Servant Leadership*:

> To be a lone chief atop a pyramid is abnormal and corrupting. None of us are perfect by ourselves, and all of us need the help and correcting influence of close colleagues. When someone is moved atop a pyramid, that person no longer has colleagues, only subordinates. Even the frankest and bravest subordinates do not talk with their boss in the same way that they talk with colleagues who are equals, and normal communication patterns become warped.[5]

When team leadership functions in a body of believers, it helps guard and promote the preeminence and position of Jesus Christ over the local church. It brings accountability and relationship to fivefold ministry leaders that building one-man ministries simply cannot. The first-century Church was Christ-centered and Christ-dependent. The centrality of Jesus Christ in all things was the fuel for the glory that they walked in on a daily basis.

DREAM WITH ME

Now I invite you to dream with me about houses of glory in the earth that have been established by apostles and where Jesus Christ is clearly the Head and foundation of the Church, rather than the gifting or charisma of one person. Imagine a body of believers who are being trained and equipped by a team of fivefold ministers so that they will become mature in Christ, not tossed back and forth by every wind of doctrine. Churches will no longer rise and fall based on the gifting and charisma of one individual, but they will be focused on Christ and equipped by fivefold ministers for the work of the Kingdom. This will bring forth the true maturity of the saints, the harvest of souls, the fathering of sons and daughters, the outpouring of the Holy Spirit, and the caring for God's people that so many long for. In the midst of global shaking, these houses of glory will emerge full of power and love.

God is releasing an apostolic blueprint and prophetic strategies to His end-time Church. We often find in Scripture that doing the right thing in the wrong way can lead to tragic results. I believe that many individuals have had a sincere burden to plant churches and establish God's Kingdom, yet they simply have not known how to pioneer true houses of glory according to the pattern revealed in the New Testament. What ends up being planted are what I call orphan churches. These are communities of believers that are being led by pastors and teachers but are disconnected from apostolic and prophetic influence and foundation.

I see God connecting these orphan churches, perhaps established with the right heart but in the wrong way, to authentic, fathering apostles and prophets. These individuals will help raise up and impart these graces so that houses of glory can truly emerge in the earth. As the biblical foundation is laid and team ministry begins to flourish, a new leadership wineskin will begin to form in the new era. It will connect with the hunger for deep relationship that God is releasing all over the earth.

NOTES

1. Wayne Grudem, *Systematic Theology* (Grand Rapids, MI: Zondervan Publishing House, 1994), 913.
2. Ibid., 931.
3. Alexander Strauch, *Biblical Eldership* (Colorado Springs, CO: Lewis and Roth Publishers, 1995), 45.
4. Ibid., 115.
5. Ibid., 41.

Chapter 5

A New Leadership Wineskin

*T*here is a hunger emerging in this generation for authentic and accountable relationships within the Body of Christ like never before. This includes a desire for church leaders to be more focused on relationship than their function or title. The fivefold ministry can no longer afford to be disconnected from the very body they are called to train and equip. This inevitably will cause a massive paradigm shift in the way both leaders and saints relate to one another. I anticipate that a religious system that has modeled itself more after the Pharisees and religious leaders than Jesus Christ will rage at this new era in the Body of Christ.

THE NEW WINESKIN IS FORMING

I recently rode in the car with a well-known minister in his early 60s. He gave me a unique perspective on this hunger for relationship and transparency. He said, "The problem with the current hunger in this generation is that they want intimate relationship, which requires too much out of church leaders. In my day, the people were satisfied with coming and watching us minister. Now the people actually want to get more involved, and it's too bad." As he said these words, I actually was overcome with grief and began to weep right in front of him. This experience as I have traveled around the world and interacted with many church leaders is not an isolated one. In fact, my heart aches and groans for so many church leaders in America and other nations (especially those in their 50s and 60s) who are set on continuing to do a model of church that has become obsolete. It worked back in the day, but those days are over. An emphasis on platforms, titles, and ministry accomplishments no longer impresses, or is even the desire, among many saints today.

I'm convinced that church leaders who refuse to drop the mic and get off a stage to learn how to actively mother and father the generations will become obsolete in the days ahead. And by obsolete, I mean out of date. I foresee many large churches shutting down and no longer being effective because they refuse to speak to the hunger that is growing like wildfire in the Body of Christ.

The "old wineskin" in the Church is currently trembling because the saints are getting over the one-man-ministry-does-all model. They are looking for fathers and mothers who are willing to roll up their sleeves and do life with them. They don't care much about the sermons anymore. They are actually looking for church leaders to model healthy marriages and what it looks like for your kids to serve the Lord with everything in them.

The "old wineskin" in the Church is confused because the saints can see through and recognize fake more than ever before. The days of plastic smiles and worshiping platform ministry are over. The living room in people's homes is now becoming the main attraction and focus. The saints are going to be taught and learn how to steward the presence of God in their homes before they ever try to welcome Him in a church service.

I'm prophesying to you that thousands of church leaders in the global Church are on the ropes, not sure if they can even keep going, because they have failed to recognize the new wineskin that is forming in the earth.

The church leaders in the days ahead who will form the new wineskin into which God will pour out the new wine (whether they are 25 or 65 years old) will model and teach true servanthood, humility that brings honor, and deep transparency and relationship. New era leaders will be accessible and not focused on platforms and microphones. They will place primary emphasis on the place of prayer and make disciples in their homes and at the dining room table.

A BOMBSHELL PHONE CONVERSATION

I had a heartbreaking phone conversation six months ago with a pastor from another state. After talking about his ministry, he asked me what my plans were for the weekend. I told him my wife and I were hosting the monthly married couples gathering at our church. We were so excited to host the thirty couples who were gathering. I told him that it was our absolute favorite gathering of the month.

He gasped on the other end of the phone. "The people in your church know where you live, Jeremiah?" he said. I admit that he totally caught me off guard. He was emphatic: "I hope you are setting boundaries between you and the people, brother. Make sure you aren't getting too close with any of the congregants or your church staff. When you build too much relationship with those you lead, they will stop honoring you. Besides, you are gaining popularity in the Body of Christ and you really need to distance yourself from the people to protect the anointing on your life."

As I listened to this pastor who had been leading the congregation he pastored for more than 25 years, my heart just grieved. I hung up the phone and just wept in my house. How does distancing ourselves from the saints as church leaders look anything like the example Jesus Christ came and gave us?

At the leading of the Holy Spirit, I actually called the pastor back later that day. He was more than twice my age. I gently said, "Brother, with all due respect, your advice to me as a young minister sounds like the Pharisees and religious leaders. Have we forgotten that one of the qualifications of being a church leader is to be hospitable? My wife and I have church members in our home three to four times a week. We see our entire church and staff we lead as a family. For us, the deeper we invest in love and relationships, the more honor we receive. I have breakfast with our elders every week and a special one-on-one with all my staff every Monday. I don't ever want to be one of those guys who has popularity and doesn't smell like sheep. I do not believe it's biblical."

There was silence on the other end of the phone. It was awkward. Then he hung up.

THE RELIGIOUS HIERARCHY MUST FALL

I truly believe the chasm that church leaders have created between themselves and the people is why so many of them are friendless, lonely, depressed, and at times suicidal. I'm convinced that the mind-set and advice given to me months ago is totally old wineskin and needs to be completely abolished in all church leadership structures. I'm so broken-hearted over how many saints have never had a meal in a fivefold minister's home, never done anything fun with them, or never known friendship with church leaders apart from ministry. I think it's totally bogus. Have we forgotten a man named Jesus Christ who came in the flesh and dwelled among the people? The Son of God humbled Himself, taking the form of a servant and being made in the likeness of humans, and built deep love and relationship with the disciples. He chose and walked with men who betrayed and left Him in His darkest hour on the cross.

Christopher Johnson pointedly speaks to this issue of religious hierarchy in the Church when he says:

In the days of Jesus Christ, the scribes and Pharisees had created for themselves a hierarchy of inequality between themselves and the people. They, as spiritual leaders, created, maintained, and enjoyed the chasm of separation between themselves and the rest of God's people. They clearly viewed themselves, based upon their positions, their titles, their education, their knowledge of God's Word, and their arrogant hearts, as a different class of people than the rest. They knew nothing of deep love and relationship with those whom they were supposedly serving and leading. Is this not the same exact description of what is taking place between spiritual leaders and saints in most of the Church today?[1]

THE EMERGENCE OF HOUSE-TO-HOUSE GATHERINGS

As we enter into this new era when houses of glory will emerge all over the earth, I see most of them popping up in neighborhoods and cities. The codependence upon large buildings and the need to be entertained by a man or a woman of God is perhaps one of the number one issues that COVID-19 has exposed in the Church.

The need for parents to disciple their own children and discover the necessity of hosting the presence of God in our homes must become a major priority in the Body of Christ.

These house-to-house gatherings will be marked by three primary realities—fire, family, and fathering. The fire of God was always meant to be stewarded in the context of a spiritual family with the oversight and care of fathers and mothers in the faith. Where there is fire (zeal, passion, and love) for Jesus among spiritual families (of all ages) with the protection and oversight of spiritual parenting, there will be a glory abiding upon the Church like never before. The depth of love between the generations will be noticed by those in the world around us. Pure and simple-hearted devotion to Jesus Christ will mark these gatherings. Fathering will heal the many wounds of so many hurting sons and daughters who do not know how to trust anymore.

A PROPHETIC WORD TO THE FIREBRANDS

"Those who carry zeal and passion for Jesus Christ and desire deep love and relationship will always look like rebellious and prideful people to church leaders who walk in insecurity and jealousy." In an open vision, I saw the spirit of Saul (insecurity and jealousy) operating through many church leaders. That spirit is currently attempting to assassinate a new breed of Davidic leaders who are crazy about the presence of Jesus and absolutely love prayer, worship, and the place of encounter. This next generation of leaders do not care who is preaching or leading so long as God manifests His glory.

I feel deeply compelled by the Spirit of God to speak a father's blessing as a leader in the Body of Christ over a new generation of firebrands. They are a generation that understands the current wineskin of the contemporary Church cannot contain the new wine God is pouring out. I declare:

> *You are not rebellious or prideful because you know there has to be more than church programs, three songs, and a nice motivational sermonette. Your concern over many church leaders who have lost the fresh anointing of the Holy Spirit because they have forgotten their first love is justified.*
>
> *Even as your heart has longed to be fathered and to be given permission to burn for Jesus, do not allow an orphan heart and a spirit of bitterness to grab hold of your heart. Yes, you are hurting and feel rejection, but as you walk in humility and allow God to heal you, He will use you in*

> *the days ahead to do the things for those you lead*
> *that your fathers refused to do for you.*

Many from this new breed of Davidic leaders and rising firebrands have not been fathered and released like they should have been because of the jealousy and insecurity of their leaders. But in the days ahead, they will move in an opposite spirit! A healthy paradigm of fathering relationships is going to emerge in this new era of glory.

NOTE

1. Christopher Johnson, *The Fullness of Ministry* (Fishnet Publications), 98.

Chapter 6

SPIRITUAL FATHERING

When Jesus said, *"Call no man your father"* (Matt. 23:9, KJV), He was not forbidding the place of spiritual fathers among His disciples. In proper context, Jesus was actually warning His disciples about the dangers of religious titles used by leaders who wanted praise and position, rather than those who humbly and lovingly served spiritual children. He was instructing His followers to avoid the kind of hypocrisy and power trip that would exalt spiritual "fathers" (and other leaders) over God as the ultimate Father. The only time having spiritual fathers is illegal in God's Kingdom is when they become idols, political positions, and preeminent over God the Father. This is why Jesus could give a warning against such titles, while Paul still called himself a "father" to the Corinthians (see 1 Cor. 4:15). The difference is, Paul used the term to describe his actual relationship to the Corinthians, not to entitle himself as a leader over them.

As long as I can remember, I have always had spiritual fathers. There have consistently been older men in my life who have provided deep love and relationship, correction, encouragement, and accountability in every season of my life and ministry. I am currently being spiritually fathered and I greatly honor and value spiritual fathers everywhere.

EXPOSING THE IDOL OF SPIRITUAL FATHERING

However, the Spirit of God has recently revealed to me a modern-day idol being erected in the Body of Christ, and it has specifically revealed itself to me as *the idol of spiritual fathering*. In other words, I believe we are watching a totally twisted, unhealthy, and perverted need for a spiritual father rising in this generation. Young and old by the thousands are attempting to find their worth, value, and significance from being connected to a spiritual father rather than knowing and understanding God *the* Father. Their ambition and motives are totally impure and polluted.

One of the truths I have learned over the years is that the primary role of true spiritual fathers is to introduce you to God *your* Father. True spiritual fathers do not make you dependent on them. They are actually more concerned that you learn to relate to *God* as your Father rather than to them as fathers.

I believe God is about to set a generation free from the idolatry of false spiritual fathering. You will see true spiritual fathers rise who actually carry a revelation of the Fatherhood of God, and they will give it away for *free*. There will be no charge to learn and grow from them as they freely give away what has been given to them. God recently said to me, "Why are so many of these people more comfortable being called a 'son' or 'daughter' by someone claiming to be an apostle than actually allowing *Me* to call them 'son' or 'daughter'?" He went on, "Why do so many of these men allow others to call them 'spiritual fathers' when they know nothing of Me as their Father? They are a bunch of orphans running around creating orphanages and charging orphans to get in!"

The idolatry of spiritual fathering is going to fall before our eyes. We have turned it into a god. It's perverted, twisted, sick, and needs to be repented of. Let's stop calling some leader "dad" and "father" because being connected to him makes us feel important. We should just save our money and get to know God as Father. Leaders, let's stop calling people who attend our churches or stay connected to our ministries our "sons" and "daughters" when we truthfully don't even know them. True spiritual fathers never seek to find their worth, value, and significance from getting as many people as possible to call them "dad." It's time for massive repentance from the idolatry of spiritual fathering. Reformation is upon us all!

SUGAR DADDY OR SPIRITUAL FATHERING

I have been overwhelmed recently by how many young people are reaching out to me regarding their longing for a "spiritual father." Upon engaging more than 50 of them in further conversation concerning what that looks like to them, I am becoming more convinced than ever that we have a millennial generation hungering for a "sugar daddy" rather than true spiritual fathering. For every cry from millennials, "Where are all the true spiritual fathers?" there could be an equally valid question: "Where are all the true spiritual sons and daughters?"

People who desire a sugar daddy are looking for a one-sided relationship where they are the benefactors. In their minds, having a spiritual father means that he pours everything he has into them at no cost on their part. They are looking for a man who will teach them everything about life and faith while they sit on the couch and take notes and make no investment in him. People who are looking for a sugar daddy do not accept correction or adjustment. They do not like the idea of having to learn, serve, and honor their spiritual father for any length of time before they go back to telling him about their problems and how they have been wronged so often in life. People who want a sugar daddy instead of a true spiritual father are searching for someone who can provide for them a platform, influence, and a greater reach than they have. Their motives are impure and sometimes evil. A true spiritual father would rebuke and confront such foolishness.

Spiritual fathers, on the other hand, are men who have deposits inside of them that people admire and even desire, but you can only access the depths of the riches living on the inside of them through deep relationship and servanthood. Someone looking for a spiritual father is not looking to be served but to serve. Someone searching for a spiritual father should desire a loving leader who can bring correction and adjustment to the parts of his or her life that are immature and out of order.

Spiritual fathers love to empower and equip. They love to challenge you and encourage you to live worthy of the call upon your life. They will faithfully remind you of the prophetic words spoken over your life and will root and ground you in the Word of God. They will listen to you, but your heart posture toward them should be quick to listen and slow to speak. My simple advice to young people searching for a true spiritual father is this: look for a man of God with whom you can build a relationship, serve him in whatever areas he needs, and make a financial investment in his life as the Holy Spirit leads. If that sounds terrible to you, then you are after a sugar daddy, not a true spiritual father. As you lay down your life, he will lay down his. Authentic relationships require time, trust, vulnerability, and sacrifice. Be patient and the fruit of a fathering relationship will come.

DENOMINATIONAL COVERING OR APOSTOLIC FATHERHOOD

The need has never been greater for men in church leadership to transition out of religious, denominational covering to true apostolic fathering. As someone who travels around the nation and the world, preaching in over 40 churches or conferences a year, and interacting closely with hundreds of church leaders throughout that time, I would say that less than ten percent of them have an active spiritual father and are being instructed, corrected, and encouraged on a weekly basis. Sure, they are part of a denominational covering, but they are lacking an intimate, vulnerable, and fathering relationship with an older man in the faith.

Meanwhile, the saints cry out for church leaders to be their spiritual fathers when church leaders themselves are not being spiritually fathered. We must cry out for this to change. We cannot give away to others what we ourselves do not possess. It is a truly heartbreaking epidemic in the Church.

Worst of all, when church leaders refuse to be fathered, the church becomes an orphanage run by orphans and the orphan spirit wreaks havoc in a generation. Remember, we teach what we know, but we reproduce who we are! We cannot merely teach about fathering. We must actually reproduce sons and daughters who one day will become fathers and mothers themselves!

APOSTOLIC CHRISTIANITY IS THE NEW WINE

Denominational structures and their institutional nature will continue to hinder and, in most cases, altogether quench the spirit of revival and awakening that is coming upon the Body of Christ. I believe a generation of Martin Luthers (reformers) is going to revolt against denominations and religious structures and form a wineskin of apostolic Christianity that will host the new wine being poured out.

Many of these leaders who carry this type of "Martin Luther" reformation anointing are currently referred to as "pastors, teachers, and evangelists" within their denominations and religious structures because there is no revelation or embracing of apostles, prophets, or apostolic Christianity. Many of these church leaders know that God has called them as apostles or prophets and is releasing them to teach apostolic Christianity straight out of the Gospels and the Book of Acts (and not from a church growth textbook), but they are unsure what will happen if they make the shift. God is going to strengthen them with the power of His might and confirm His Word.

The Holy Spirit has been specifically highlighting five states to me—Texas, North Carolina, Alabama, Tennessee, and Mississippi—as states where reformation is about to take place within denominations and religious structures. The religious spirit is going to attack, accuse, and operate in political games like never before, but the Spirit of God is going to oversee this entire paradigm shift and reformation as apostolic Christianity is restored to the Church.

Remember, in 1517 Martin Luther nailed the paper containing his 95 theses to the church doors in Wittenberg. All he sought was a debate, but little did he know he was starting a fire that would burn through the ages! The language of "apostolic Christianity" is more than a debate; we are talking about a fire that is going to burn through denominations and religious structures forever.

APOSTOLIC GRACE OR MCDONALD'S FRANCHISING

One of the primary functions of apostolic grace is the fathering and eventually sending/releasing of sons and daughters to plant churches and make disciples. This mandate requires deep relationship, which often takes *years*. Learning, maturing, receiving correction, working through disagreements, and catching the heart and passion of a father is a lengthy process that needs adequate time to develop.

It is also within the sphere of apostolic grace to establish God's Kingdom, which at times includes the planting of churches. Apostles can plant churches and also commission sons and daughters to do the same, but the key ingredient here is that in order for apostolic grace to function biblically, there must be true fathering taking place. What is fathering if you're not starting families? I'll give you an example. Several years ago, I spoke to a man who claimed to be an apostle and said he had planted 9 churches and he was only 35 years old. I did recognize apostolic grace on him, but I also asked him why he was franchising like McDonald's. Upset, he asked me what I meant and I explained to him what I wrote above.

If an apostle has not actually fathered sons and daughters who were sent to plant churches (which takes years), he has a bunch of McDonald's franchises that are puffing him up rather than doing the hard labor of true apostolic ministry.

THE APOSTOLIC TRAIN DECEPTION

To have friends and leaders who like your church model, then ask to join your network, and then call their church by the same name as yours *in no way represents apostolic grace*. Neither are you their spiritual father; you are simply a regional manager who oversees franchisees. Claiming to be an apostle with nine churches with the same name, when you did not labor and take the years required to actually father sons and daughters, in no way represents apostolic grace. It makes you really good at franchising your network or church like McDonald's, though.

Be on the lookout for "apostles" who make huge claims of planting x number of churches and having x numbers of sons and daughters when the truth is that they have not spent the *years* of investment or requirements to actually produce apostolic fruit. There are lots of great "apostolic" McDonald's franchises out there in the American Church, but very few legitimate apostles who have sent true sons and daughters to plant and establish the Kingdom of God.

THE APOSTOLIC NETWORKING MERRY-GO-ROUND

I recently received a very powerful prophetic dream where God said to me, "My people must be warned of the coming apostolic merry-go-round. In the days of Paul, some claimed to be of Cephas and others of Apollos, yet it is no different in the days that you are living in. False allegiance to man is what has caused the immaturity of much of the apostolic ministry in America."

We are living in a day and age when in order to be a spiritual son or daughter to many so-called apostles, one must pay monthly dues or be labeled "false sons and daughters." In other words, these "apostles" are asking people to rent their name per month so that they can declare that they are operating under "apostolic covering and authority." I call it "Rent-a-Daddy." Through fear, intimidation, and control, the apostolic networking merry-go-round is being established and advanced in America. In a gifted generation that is truly hungering for fathering, they are being prostituted and pimped and many don't even know it. If anyone dares to challenge these so-called apostles, they will be blacklisted and the minions working in these networks will be told not to associate with these individuals. A secret society is being formed within these networks that more resembles the mob than the Bride of Christ.

Unfortunately, in order to preserve their public image and reputation, these "apostles" will only network with certain individuals from whom they can benefit. It's all about money, applause, public image, and opportunistic relationships. The larger your platform and influence, the more you have to offer these "apostles." I'm convinced many of those posing as these types of "apostles" should really just go open up a multi-level marketing business in the world. That way they can stop ruining authentic apostolic ministry, which is based on sincere love and relationship without financial cost and without the political trade-off of platforms and "open doors."

I believe the primary reason God is sounding the alarm about the rise of apostolic network merry-go-rounds is because Jesus is being sold out and merchandised. "Apostolic ministry" has turned into a marketplace for prostitution and casual harlotry. May the true apostolic fathers rise in this generation—fathers who don't need networks to validate themselves. And may sons and daughters stop settling for cheap networking techniques and strategies that will eventually leave them more orphaned than they were before.

HEALTHY AND UNHEALTHY SPIRITUAL FATHERING

Healthy spiritual fathers *correct* and *commission*, but they do not *compete* with sons and daughters. King Saul is an example of an extremely dysfunctional and unhealthy spiritual father who competed with young David rather than correct and commission him. The song that said, *"Saul has slain his thousands, and David his tens of thousands"* (1 Sam. 18:7) should have produced great joy in Saul. But because of his own insecurity and jealousy—the bad fruits of competition—he simply did not know how to father properly. In light of this current pattern, I offer this prophetic encouragement and strong warning:

> *There are **many** men in their late 40s, 50s, and 60s who were never fathered spiritually in a healthy way, yet they seek to father the next generation. Because they were never properly corrected and commissioned themselves, they will compete with sons and daughters who begin to gain influence and anointing. (I have seen this in the Kingdom of God **more** than anything else so far.) They either accuse younger ministers of arrogance and pride, or they seek to dominate them altogether. They will continually hear the success of the next generation as a challenge to their own desires to succeed.*

TRUE SPIRITUAL FATHERING

"The absence of genuine affection from spiritual fathers to sons and daughters is one of the greatest deficits in God's Kingdom." Without deep relationship and vulnerability from spiritual fathers, the sons and daughters go wild looking for affirmation and acceptance in all the wrong places. Do you have a spiritual father who is available to go to lunch and talk about life, or do you have a spiritual father with whom everything you talk about is centered around ministry?

The spirit of competition that operates among so many ministers in the Kingdom is one of the number one signs that true spiritual fathering is not taking place. Even a secular psychologist can tell you that there is no room for competition in a family. We have created a twisted system in the Church and on social media, where sons and daughters strive for personal achievement, promotion, and individual advancement—all signs that true spiritual fathering is absent.

Sons and daughters who are being spiritually fathered in healthy ways are content in who God has called them to be and do not constantly compete against others for the platform and notoriety. When you are around sons and daughters who are being fathered well, you sense peace, not pressure. They know their identity and don't have anything to prove. Oh, how this generation of sons and daughters could be transformed with proper fathering and discipleship.

As a pioneer church planter, I know the frustrations of local ministry. And as a traveling prophetic minister, I constantly hear the disappointment of pastors, leaders, and worship leaders from around the country. They have expectations of church members that quite frankly hardly ever get met. We want church members to attend more services, we want the guitar player to value excellence more, we want the greeters to actually smile and not look half asleep, we wonder if anyone is really listening to our preaching, we're interested to know if the congregation really does enjoy our worship leading, and we want to know where everyone is when the prayer meetings take place. The list goes on and on.

In the midst of these mullings, pressures, frustrations, and disappointments, the voice of the Holy Spirit has been so faithful for many years to communicate *the same message* to me every time. He says, "Jeremiah, how will they understand unless you model for them what you want from them? Jeremiah, how will they 'get it' unless you make the sacrifice to teach, show, demonstrate, train, and equip?"

Oh, the tension! The heart of true fathering and mothering is not just to release with our words what we expect from others, but actually to demonstrate, model, train, equip, and—most of all—get off the pedestal. Truth be told, the most frustrated and disappointed leaders I know from around the country are doing nothing to train and equip those under them who are struggling. They think that by continuing to communicate their expectations, people will magically get it one day, or God will send them some all-star lineup that does not need leaders to pour into them.

The difference between leaders who merely lead and leaders who carry the heart of the Father is found in what happens beyond their words. Leaders who lead only know how to "tell people what to do." Leaders who carry the heart of the Father show, demonstrate, and model for those they serve what they want to see, and they are willing to labor with the weak to see them made strong! In essence, the heart of true fathering/mothering is found in the commitment to model, train, and equip!

If the flock is not supernatural enough for you—*train them, equip them, and model practical faith and miracles for them.*

If the worship team isn't skilled enough for you—*train them, equip them, and model hard work and dedication for them.*

If the leadership team lacks character—*train, equip, and model integrity for them.*

If the church lacks volunteers—*train, equip, and model sacrificial service for them.*

If marriages and families are broken—*train, equip, and model healthy marriage and family for them.*

A VISION OF THE DAYS AHEAD

The need for spiritual fathering in the Body of Christ has never been greater. I see men and women emerging who will be accessible, humble, and full of the love of God the Father for His children. I believe this generation is destined to be fathered by men who can't give them a platform, but who *can* impart a deeper love and correction than they have ever known. True spiritual fathers pray for you and have your spiritual growth in Christ as their primary concern (see Gal. 4:19).

For three years in Ephesus, Paul never ceased personally warning and exhorting the elders of the church, night and day, and with tears (see Acts 20:31). And when he met them at Miletus to bid them all farewell, they all wept as they embraced and kissed him (see Acts 20:37-38). They loved Paul and knew him to be a true father who loved them. This is what authentic apostolic fatherhood is all about. Cheap networking and marketing schemes will never replace the need for deep relationship among saints and spiritual fathers.

If you are not currently being spiritually fathered, I want to encourage you to make this a priority in prayer. But do not seek to force a relationship with a leader that is just not there. Also, make sure you are clear regarding your expectations. I meet too many people who desire a sit-down lunch every week with a leader who has a national traveling ministry. As I have stated earlier, much of the disappointment involving spiritual fathering is that those who desire it are really seeking someone who in their view is famous or has a platform. I would even highly recommend that those who have a high profile in the Body of Christ actually need to be fathered by a man who does not have a similar sphere of influence. This will enable the fathering relationship to be based on the most important issues such as personal character and a healthy marriage, not platform status.

The healthiest fathering relationships are organic and take time. Communication and realistic expectations are necessary for growth. A heart posture to serve and honor is key for those desiring to be fathered. Likewise, a grace to love, correct, and encourage is required on the part of those fathering. The fire of God was always meant to be stewarded in the context of a spiritual family with the oversight of fathers. Where there is fire (zeal, passion, love) for Jesus among spiritual families (consisting of all ages), with the protection and oversight of spiritual fathers, there will be a glory abiding upon the house of God never seen before. The depth of love between the generations will be noticed by those in the world around us. Pure, simple-hearted devotion to Jesus Christ will mark these types of gatherings. True spiritual fathering will heal the many wounds of hurting sons and daughters.

THE POWER OF SPIRITUAL MOTHERING

While I have spent considerable time emphasizing the need for spiritual fathering in this chapter, I also do not want to minimize the impact that spiritual mothers have had in my life. I have had the privilege of walking with spiritual fathers in the last 12 years of full-time ministry. They have faithfully rebuked me, corrected me, and encouraged me in very critical seasons of my life. They bring authority, tenacity, and a boldness that I have learned to respect and honor with the highest regard.

With that being said, I never properly learned the value of spiritual mothers until five years ago. They are precious gifts from the Father who impart treasure and discernment that you could never receive from spiritual fathers. If you do not know the difference between spiritual fathers and mothers, you are seriously missing out.

Recently I was battling some very serious spiritual warfare. I had not slept more than three hours on consecutive nights of ministry due to wrestling with a principality over the Midwest. I was being tormented and quite frankly was worn out. My prophetic nature in these moments is to be strong and put my armor on for another war. It's the valuable lessons I've learned from spiritual fathers that has kept me strong in battle.

However, God knew exactly what I needed when I arrived to my next destination to minister. Two spiritual mothers arrived to the meeting and immediately picked up on my distress. They began to pray for me and I experienced the tangible love, tenderness, and compassionate nurturing I needed to recharge. Their calm and reassuring words brought life to my soul and broke the accusations of the devil off my mind and heart. I learned that sometimes in the midst of the battles, God has a storehouse of spiritual fathers and mothers who will impart to us exactly what we need.

A PROPHETIC WORD OF RELEASE

The Spirit of God would say:

> *I bless this generation to be spiritually fathered and mothered by truly godly people who do not have a nationally recognized name or platform. Oh, how My heart aches for so many fathers and mothers in this hour whom I have put a rich deposit of Myself inside. They are constantly overlooked by young ones because they are not*

popular or visible in My body. There is an insidious and destructive hunger in this generation to be connected to famous leaders that breaks My heart. I release you from these vain imaginations and bless you to honor, submit, serve, and build relationship with the wise and mature fathers and mothers around you.

Chapter 7

Upper Room DNA

*H*ouses of glory are emerging in the earth that are built on the foundation of Jesus Christ and established by apostles and prophets—the foundational ministries (see Eph. 2:20). Pastors, teachers, and evangelists (building ministries) will labor together so that all five ministries might train and equip the saints for the work of ministry like never before. We will see a tremendous increase in humility and maturity in the Body of Christ as this starts to take place. Indeed, a biblical wineskin is forming that is established on team ministry, family, and fathering.

One of the most essential qualities of a house of glory is the atmosphere—the spiritual temperature—it creates in partnership with the Spirit. I call this "Upper Room DNA." Entertainment worship and powerless prayer will never function inside a true house of glory. The first-century Church in the Book of Acts was birthed from an upper room encounter and must be seen as a blueprint for true Kingdom witness (see Acts 2). Francis Chan correctly identifies this woeful shift from the biblical model that has taken place in many churches when he says:

> The benchmark of success in church services has become more about attendance than the movement of the Holy Spirit. The "entertainment" model of church was largely adopted in the 1980s and '90s, and while it alleviated some of our boredom for a couple of hours a week, it filled our churches with self-focused consumers rather than self-sacrificed servants attuned to the Holy Spirit.[1]

THE TABERNACLE OF DAVID

In Acts 15 at the Jerusalem Council, James declared that, according to Amos 9:11, a day would come when God would rebuild and restore the fallen Tabernacle of David, which is a type and shadow of Christ and His Church. It is this vision of having unlimited access, without the curtain and veil, that beckons the New Testament Church into the deeper waters of true prayer and worship. Vertical prayer and worship actually kill the entertainment spirit in the Church because it invites people to engage Jesus Christ upon the throne rather than a worship leader on a stage.

Corporate worship was never intended to be a means to preaching. Rather, worship is an end in itself. We were created to give glory, honor, and praise to Jesus Christ. The entertainment model of church creates meetings where people are taught how to attend services rather than move in the power and gifts of the Holy Spirit.

The ministries of apostles and prophets are so Christ-centered that they cannot function properly in a house where the worship and prayer is man-centered. When worship songs and intercession are focused on self-gratification and personal needs, it will disrupt the grace and anointing that God has placed on His foundation-layers. Apostles and prophets refuse to pioneer without the glory of God. They are allergic to environments where catering to the needs of people is the top priority.

Apostles and prophets are presence-based, not program-driven. Their expertise is in taking dead, dry, religious organizations and cities and turning them into Spirit-filled, fiery, life-giving organisms and regions. The Upper Room DNA—a sharp focus on vertical worship and prayer—is the right atmosphere and goal of apostles and prophets. The entertainment model of church has effectively suffocated the life out of young, upcoming apostles and prophets. However, God's answer in an hour of crisis is always to provide solutions to His remnant—houses of glory for a new era!

CORPORATE PRAYER AND INTERCESSION

As a church planter and traveling prophetic minister in the Body of Christ, I place a high value on attendance at corporate prayer gatherings to define the success— the actual fruit—among a community of believers. The early Church in the Book of Acts was birthed from a corporate prayer meeting (the upper room) and also sustained by corporate prayer meetings (house to house and the temple). In the words of Leonard Ravenhill, "Sunday morning church attendance shows how popular the church is; Sunday night shows how popular the preacher is; and attendance at prayer meetings shows how popular God is."

I appreciate conferences and Sunday morning church services, but houses of glory learn how to pray and contend without a celebrity personality or hype. They have been captivated by the Audience of One! I'm convinced that we have many popular preachers and ministries around the world, but we have a God in Heaven who has largely been forgotten. We must repent! We also must have more preachers and ministries calling saints to prayer meetings or even attending them. As one preacher told me, "If we have a conference on revival, everyone comes. But if we have a conference on prayer, no one shows up." I looked at him and said, "Well, there is no such thing as real revival without prayer." He was stunned. As long as prayer rooms are empty during the week while Sunday morning services are filled, we will never have a Third Great Awakening. Corporate prayer and worship must be restored to the Body of Christ.

Countless diversions have distracted church leaders from their biblical mandate to put primary emphasis on prayer and the study of God's Word. Mike Bickle has accurately stated, "The greatest disease in church leadership today is leaders in the Body of Christ who have no time or desire for prayerful, long, and loving mediation on the Word of God." Church leaders should be attending or leading several prayer meetings a week at their church.

Nothing irritates me more than to hear how incredibly hard people work in a community of believers for their income, only to find out that part of their tithe and offering is going to support church leaders who are not giving themselves fully to prayer and the study of God's Word. It is not acceptable, and should not be tolerated, when church leaders work two or three days per week, have no disciplined life of prayer and fasting, and preach without the anointing because they simply don't seek God. Church members should expect that their church leaders live a life of prayer and carry a fresh word from their time spent in the Upper Room each week.

ELIMINATING INTERCESSORS AND PROPHETIC GROUPS

When church leadership does not attend, lead, or interact with intercessory and prophetic groups in their midst, they silence their most reliable sources of discernment and revelation. When this happens, a spiritual vacuum is created and the spirit of Jezebel will begin her disgusting work. Alarmed, many intercessors and prophetic people will begin to warn the leadership of Jezebel and her schemes.

Sadly, if they continue to operate in ignorance, or just plain refuse to listen, they will actually become a kindred spirit with Jezebel. Unknowingly or knowingly, they will align themselves with her (see Rev. 2:20). Without repentance from church leadership for falling into this trap, they will become puppet leaders subject to strong delusion, heavy depression, and an inability to make necessary decisions concerning the spiritual atmosphere of the church.

Even worse than this, spiritual famine will begin to descend upon ministries where church leadership refuses to deal with and confront Jezebel and her schemes. God's manifest presence will begin to fade from the atmosphere, and, sadly, most leaders will not even recognize this as God's judgment. Jezebel wants intercessory and prophetic groups shut down immediately from churches and does not want church leaders to attend any of these meetings where they can receive discernment and revelation from those God has sent them to encourage and warn them. The spirit of Jezebel will either shut down prayer meetings or desire to control and lead the prayer meetings.

If true prophetic intercession is not taking place behind the scenes in your church, or the leadership is not attending any of these meetings, it's a dead giveaway that the spirit of Jezebel is most likely at work in your midst.

CULTIVATING PRAYER AND WORSHIP

There is no such thing as authentic apostolic and pro-phetic churches, nor true apostles and prophets, that do not place primary emphasis on prayer and worship. This is because the spirit of revelation such churches and leaders should carry and release can only be accessed in the secret place. The lack of a strong per-sonal prayer life or prayer culture among individuals and churches claiming "apostolic or prophetic" any-thing is clear evidence that they are either ignorant or deceived of what they are claiming to possess.

We must have a generation of apostles and apostolic churches that pray in tongues "more" than those who merely claim to be Spirit-filled (see 1 Cor. 14:18), and we must have a generation of prophets and prophetic churches that make intercession to the Lord of Hosts without ceasing (see Jer. 27:18; 1 Thess. 5:17). An "apos-tle" or "prophet" who leads an apostolic or prophetic church yet does not have a strong prayer culture or seri-ous emphasis on the secret place is simply not a biblical apostle or prophet. Let's humble ourselves and return back to the Word of God. We must have an Ephesians 1:17 mandate restored back to the global Church!

Paul and the other apostles did not establish Sunday morning church services with a midweek Bible study or home gathering and call it a church plant. They planted houses of encounter where prayer and worship to Jesus Christ took preeminence above all other religious activity. This is why Jesus referred to His Father's house as a "house of prayer" (Mark 11:17).

Be on the lookout for houses of glory to emerge all over the earth—houses with an atmosphere filled with the fresh fragrance of true worshipers who are not there to be entertained but rather to pour out their adoration before Yahweh. Their focus will be fixed on the One who sits on the throne, not their favorite worship leader and band. A lovesickness for the Bridegroom is going to move upon the Bride that will override the order of service. Days are coming when the beckoning call from the Holy Spirit to ascend into the Upper Room will be so great that calendars and clocks will no longer matter. "As houses of glory become presence-based rather than program-based, the gifts of the Holy Spirit will begin to function among the people of God like never before." It's going to be glorious!

NOTE

1. Francis Chan, *Forgotten God* (Colorado Springs, CO: David C. Cook, 2009), 15-16.

Chapter 8

THE EXPLOSION OF THE GIFTS

I graduated with honors from the largest Pentecostal university in the United States. I have also preached to date in more than three hundred Spirit-filled churches all over America and the world. Attendance at these meetings has ranged from fifty members to more than ten thousand on many occasions. I have interacted with and ministered for some of the most well-known Pentecostal theologians, Charismatic pastors with doctorate degrees, and even some "Spirit-filled" itinerant ministers who, based on my observations, did not seem to have even heard of Azusa Street.

From my personal experience with a Pentecostal education and ministering extensively in so many

Charismatic churches, I can say this without hesitation: at least 75 percent of them have been totally dominated by religious rhetoric with little to no evidence of the Holy Spirit's actual presence and movement. Yes, I just said that—emphatically.

My Pentecostal school experience left me terrified that a generation of future, Spirit-filled ministers did not pray in tongues daily, nor did they operate in any gifts of the Spirit. Several years ago, I was invited as a guest lecturer at a Pentecostal university in a room full of college seniors. By a show of hands, all 42 of them intended to pursue full-time ministry upon graduation. When I asked them how many actively spoke in tongues and operated in the gifts of the Holy Spirit, only three of them raised their hands! I started weeping on the spot. Where have the active miracles, prophecy, tongues, fiery prayer meetings, and power evangelism gone in the Charismatic and Pentecostal movements these days?

To some of the Spirit-filled preachers reading this who know I'm writing the truth, yet all of your buildings and boards have been overtaken by religion, I say this: it could be time to wake yourself up and start walking with the Holy Spirit again. To those Spirit-filled saints attending seeker-sensitive or flat-out dry churches, I say this: stop complaining and get praying. Corporate revival is birthed from personal revival. Stop rotting on the pew in the back and get up to the frontlines of the prayer altar—and press in.

INSTRUCTIONS FOR CORPORATE GATHERINGS

There is no place in the Scriptures that definitively explains or commands what should happen when saints gather in the name of the Lord Jesus. The Bible does not list three songs, an offering, and a short message as the requirements for the assembling of believers. We all have to ask ourselves where we developed a theology for the house of God that prefers spectating and entertainment over participation involving real glory and encounters.

The Bible addresses some of the specifics of corporate gatherings in Hebrews 10:25 and First Corinthians 14:26. Hebrews 10:25 says, *"Not forsaking our own assembling together, as is the habit of some, but encouraging one another; and all the more as you see the day drawing near."* And First Corinthians 14:26 says, *"What is the outcome then, brethren? When you assemble, each one has a psalm, has a teaching, has a revelation, has a tongue, has an interpretation. Let all things be done for edification.*" Considering these two texts, we can acknowledge then that the Scriptures command us not to forsake gathering together in Hebrews 10:25 and offers multiple suggestions for what can happen when the saints gather in First Corinthians 14:26.

THE ONE-MAN MINISTRY

The New Testament explicitly empowers and encourages the saints to recognize that they are the dwelling place of God, the temple of the Holy Spirit. They are called to be ministers of reconciliation and messengers of the good news. In too much of the global Church, instead of empowering the saints, we have used them as pew fodder for a select group of gifted and talented men and women. This paradigm for ministry is not only absent in the New Testament, but is *opposed* to the New Testament—and it is oppressive in nature.

Biblical scholar William Barclay, commenting on First Corinthians 14:26, says:

> There was obviously a flexibility about the order of service in the early Church. Everything was informal enough to allow any man who felt that he had a message to give to give it. It may well be that we set far too much store on

dignity and order nowadays, and have become the slaves of orders of service. The really notable thing about an early Church service must have been that almost everyone came feeling that he had both the privilege and the obligation of contributing something to it. A man did not come with the sole intention of being a passive listener; he came not only to receive but to give. Obviously this had its dangers, for it is clear that in Corinth there were those who were too fond of the sound of their own voices; but nonetheless the Church must have been in those days much more the real possession of the ordinary Christian. It may well be that the Church lost something when she delegated so much to the professional ministry and left so little to the ordinary church member.[1]

PARTICIPANTS OR SPECTATORS

Upon entering a gathering of believers in the first-century Church, all of the saints would have been expected to contribute to the meeting in some way. Paul put it like this: *"When you assemble, each one has a psalm, has a teaching, has a revelation, has a tongue, has an interpretation"* (1 Cor. 14:26). The atmosphere Paul describes authorizes and expects believers to participate rather than spectate, and engage rather than observe. I firmly believe that if Paul—or any member of the first-century Church—walked into the majority of services conducted by the modern, global Church, he would be astounded to see them run by one pastor or a very small group of hand-selected leaders.

THE SIZE OF THE CHURCH

Many will argue that the size of the churches they attend does not allow or make room for Paul's instructions in First Corinthians 14:26. They will also say that the gatherings of the first-century Church were much smaller than they are today. These two points are valid and need careful consideration.

I do agree that the sheer size of many churches today would make it impossible to facilitate First Corinthians 14:26 meetings on Sunday mornings. There is just no way that everyone, or even a majority of people, could participate and contribute in some way. While the size of a church can hinder the potential move of the Spirit, there still could be staff members, elders, or deacons entrusted to operate in the gifts of the Spirit. Unfortunately, too many large congregations are more concerned with how long services are than what God wants in that particular meeting. Clocks have killed more moves of the Spirit than demons ever will.

If First Corinthians 14:26 meetings were an intricate part of New Testament Christianity, and the church is too large to facilitate them on Sunday mornings, why aren't these types of meetings at least taking place throughout the congregation during the week from house to house?

What about smaller churches? The average church in America only has approximately eighty members. Surely these meetings are not too large for some expression of First Corinthians 14:26 to take place! Why are we so dependent upon one man or woman to tell us what God is saying when we have equal access to the Father as well?

FACILITATING FIRST CORINTHIANS 14:26 MEETINGS

If we believe that the New Testament gives us liberty in guiding and directing what happens when saints gather together, no matter how large or small the attendance, how can we facilitate these gatherings in a way that is edifying to all those who are present? Having the ability to control and order church meetings will ensure fewer surprises by saints who potentially believe they have something to contribute. But church leaders who want to see more movement of the Holy Spirit in their midst have some reasonable fears: "What if someone says something stupid? What if someone talks too long? Will I be criticized for not having control of the meeting? Will some of the members leave the fellowship because they want more structure and order?" But in response, the one question such leaders must answer is this: "Are we seeking to please man or please God?" If a church leader believes he is the main person with an anointing—if he believes he possesses the most experience, has the greatest revelation, or is the most righteous in the group—then he will probably never be interested in what anyone else has to contribute.

It's helpful, if possible, to have someone facilitate gatherings that encourage the release of the gifts of the Holy Spirit. On a Sunday morning, an elder or someone who has been given authority by the leadership should be consulted before gifts are released. Remember, exercising the spiritual gifts is about seeking to edify one another in love. Paul also said to "know those who labor among you," which can be applied to the potential issues that can arise when individuals whom spiritual leaders are not familiar with begin ministering in to a congregation. Establishing relationship is always the key to seeing the gifts of the Holy Spirit operate unhindered. Here are some qualities I have noted over the years of individuals who excel in helping to facilitate what God wants to do in a gathering of believers.

Eight Qualities of Great Facilitators

Great facilitators:

1. Possess humility.

2. Have a sincere desire to see others share what they have received from the Lord.

3. Do not want to use their role as a platform to preach.

4. Benefit from a sound background in biblical studies and theology.

5. Possess a heart and attitude of love.

6. Go into meetings without trying to have one of their personal needs met.

7. Are sensitive to their comments, facial expressions, and body language when they respond to others.

8. Are able to correct and instruct if necessary.

WHAT CAN HAPPEN IN
FIRST CORINTHIANS 14:26 MEETINGS

These types of meetings can include prayer for healing, different types of prayer or declarations, prophecy (corporate and individually), a teaching, miracles, testimonies, songs, drawing or painting, silence, Spirit baptisms, calls for salvation, Lord's Supper, praying for people going into ministry, and the laying on of hands. Paul encouraged all things to be done in order for the edification of the body of believers.

The mind-set going into First Corinthians 14:26 meetings is to be filled with excitement and wonder over what the Holy Spirit is about to do in your midst. There are hundreds and thousands of gifted, anointed believers who never have the opportunity to express what God has deposited within them, either on a Sunday morning or in a house setting. "If believers knew that they were expected to attend corporate gatherings with something to contribute, wouldn't they spend more time with God during the week, asking Him to speak to them?" One reason so many believers have a shallow experience of God is because they are so dependent on a leader (or a few leaders) for their spiritual growth, and they know little to nothing will be expected of them when they come to church gatherings. In such settings, "church" actually molds God's people into passive spectators rather than active body members (disciples)—which is the reverse of what Scripture teaches Church should be.

CONFRONTING RELIGIOUS TRADITIONS

Where human religious traditions govern church services, everything is scripted, preplanned, and methodically carried out. There is no room for anything spontaneous, Spirit-filled, or shifting of the service in nature because those actions cannot be controlled or predicted. Religious traditions thrive on what can be controlled, predicted, and expected. These kinds of church services end before they begin because they are that robotic and mechanical.

The ministry of the Holy Spirit is the number one enemy of the religious traditions of men. It brings spontaneity, fresh vision, and unpredictability to church services, which makes the church leaders and saints who operate in a religious spirit very uncomfortable. When worship leaders stop singing the words on the screen and sing a spontaneous song to the Lord, religious traditions are challenged. When men and women of God preach under a strong prophetic anointing that challenges structures and systems, religious traditions become very upset. When saints prepare to participate at corporate gatherings rather than be entertained, religious traditions become afraid.

The unbelievable thing to me is that half the church leaders and saints who reject the types of thoughts I just wrote above actually claim to be "Spirit-filled." The truth is that in many churches we have regulated the ministry of the Holy Spirit to the sign out by our roads, but He hasn't moved in our midst in years! How can we profess to be "Pentecostal" or "Charismatic" while nothing in our church services says so? During my ten years of planting a church and leading corporate services with hundreds of people, I never once created an "order of service." We never put a single clock in our sanctuary. Our services were never a free-for-all but rather a safe place where the Spirit of God could move with order and edification.

Houses of glory are emerging in the earth where the atmosphere created by the vertical worship will beckon the Holy Spirit to begin to move among the saints like never before. Time restraints and drive-through mentalities will never work in a true house of glory. The sound in these houses will never be dominated by one man's voice, but by a family of believers who are working together in the Spirit with the fivefold ministry. Church leaders and saints will partner together to create houses of glory all over the earth. Fivefold ministers will train and equip the saints for ministry and create environments for the gifts of the Holy Spirit to flow like never before.

NOTE

1. William Barclay, *William Barclay's Daily Study Bible,* "1 Corinthians 14," Practical Advice (ii), Studylight .org, https://www.studylight.org/commentaries/ dsb/1-corinthians-14.html.

Chapter 9

BEWARE OF THE ACCUSER

*J*n Revelation 12:10, a loud voice in Heaven declares, *"Now the salvation, and the power, and the kingdom of our God and the authority of His Christ have come, for the accuser of our brethren has been thrown down, he who accuses them before our God day and night."* What a beautiful description of the dominion of Jesus Christ being spread out all over the earth! However, we must take special notice that the salvation, power, Kingdom, and authority of God will never be established *until* the accuser of the brethren has been cast down.

Since the days of my youth, I have been surrounded by saints who have desired a greater expression of God's Kingdom upon the earth. Whether we cried out for revival or the miraculous, the hunger has always been present. However, hiding deep within the hearts of too many churches and individuals is a spirit of accusation that comes to sabotage the move of the Holy Spirit in our midst. In fact, the number one enemy of a house of glory for a new era is the spirit of accusation that will seek to stir up strife, division, and chaos among God's people.

CLEAN OUT THE FILTER

If love is the heart posture in which we must exercise the gifts of the Spirit, then every sin or offense we refuse to deal with and repent of will not only hinder but distort the purity of the spiritual gifts we have been given.

For example, Susie receives a powerful prophetic word of blessing and encouragement for Bob. However, she finds Bob annoying when he worships and rude when he talks to children in the church, so she is offended by him. If Susie does not address the bitterness and resentment in her heart toward Bob, the word of blessing and encouragement the Spirit wants her to give Bob will be tainted by her personal opinions or, worse, hindered from release at all.

Another example would be that Billy is impressed by the Lord to give a financial gift to Wendy who cannot pay her bills. The problem is that Billy thinks Wendy is a poor steward of her finances and a terrible mother to her two children. If Billy does not deal with and address the criticism and negativity in his heart toward Wendy, Billy will most likely either not give to her at all, thus disobeying the prompting of the Lord, or give to her spitefully and not receive a reward from God.

The strength of a judgmental and accusatory spirit is the lack of face-to-face interaction between the two parties involved. Offense is always looking to grow and increase among believers who refuse to build relationship with one another. In communities of believers who fail to develop vulnerable and honest relationships, the spirits of accusation and fault-finding will grow in strength. If you are involved in relationships where you cannot share how and why you feel about certain issues, they are unhealthy and dysfunctional.

THE WEAPON OF PRAYER

One of the strongest weapons against the accuser of the brethren and fault-finding spirits is the weapon of prayer and intercession. Francis Frangipane skillfully describes how these spirits operate:

> The faultfinder demon will incite individuals to spend days and even weeks unearthing

old faults or sins in their minister or church. The people held captive by this deceitful spirit become "crusaders," irreconcilable enemies of their former assemblies. In most cases, the things they deem wrong or lacking are the very areas in which the Lord seeks to position them for intercession. What might otherwise be an opportunity for spiritual growth and meeting a need becomes an occasion of stumbling and withdrawal. In truth, their criticisms are a smoke screen for a prayerless heart and an unwillingness to serve.[1]

The spirits of accusation and fault-finding must be replaced with prayer and a love that covers a multitude of sins. "God could very well be showing you the sins of others. But He does not reveal them as ammunition for criticism; He reveals them so you can pray for and love them!" Are you surprised by what you see in others? Look in the mirror. You don't have it all together either.

FALSE DISCERNMENT

If we are ever going to exercise the true spiritual gift of distinguishing of spirits, we are going to have to crucify our instincts to judge and criticize others. We must uproot thought systems that have not been planted in the divine soil of faith and love.

Without divine forgiveness constantly working in our hearts, we will exercise the spiritual gifts God has given us from the place of deception. We will believe we are moving in discernment when in truth we are operating in an accusing and fault-finding spirit. Discovering the imperfections of a church leader, church, or church member is by no means a sign of spiritual maturity. We could do that even before we were Christians. What we do with what we see, however, reveals the measure of Christ-like maturity we carry. Remember, when Jesus saw the condition of humanity, He did not judge and accuse us. He died to take away our sins.

Our thoughts and heart attitudes toward fellow members of Christ's body should always be *"faith working through love"* (Gal. 5:6). Remember, satan never offers grace nor extends mercy for repentance to anyone. His goal is to harm, not heal—to accuse, not reconcile. When addressing sin in one another, we have to ask ourselves, what is the goal or aim? If it is not restoration and redemption, we may be operating in a demonic spirit that deeply grieves the heart of God.

THE REBUKER SYNDROME

There are some members of the Body of Christ who believe their job is to bring rebuke and correction to anyone or anything in the church that is not operating according to what they believe is a biblical standard. They spend more time preying on the saints than praying for the saints, and they typically move on from one group to another if their accusations and assessments are ignored or they aren't taken seriously. These people are obsessed with the dysfunction in others and can rarely see their own. They leap at the first sight of a perceived problem that they believe they are called to expose, and they let everyone know about it. Beware, they come to hurt, not heal, and destroy, not bring life. Like the Pharisees, they are hard on everyone else and easy on their own character issues. Do you have an issue with your brother and sister in your church community? Stop talking about them and go straight to them (see Matt. 18:15)! The offspring of the spirits of accusation and fault-finding are gossip and slander.

WHEN SAINTS HAVE SIN IN THEIR LIVES

We all need correction in our lives, but the ministry of reproof must be patterned after Jesus Christ and not the accuser of the brethren. If the word of rebuke or correction does not offer hope and opportunity for repentance, it's not the voice of Jesus Christ! Galatians 6:1 establishes clear protocol for addressing sin in the life of another member of the Body of Christ. We are to go to him in a spirit of gentleness. We address him with humility, while examining our own lives. Finally, we check our motives to make sure they are pure and in pursuit of restoration.

To be truly equipped to bring Christ-like corrections to a church or individual, we must also be equipped with Christ's motives. We will always be serving in churches where something is wrong. No church is perfect. Our response to what we see defines how Christ-like we actually are. If we see weakness in the Body of Christ, our call is to supply strength. Where we see sin, our response is to exemplify virtue. When we discover fear, we must impart courage. And where there is worldliness, we must display holiness. Our assignment is to enter the place of need and stand there until the Body of Christ is healed in that area.

The truth is that the Lord has intentionally placed us in a world and church community that is imperfect. Where we see something that is less than Christ, we are also seeing our opportunity to become Christ-like. The Lord doesn't want us to complain that the nursery carpet is dirty; He wants us to clean the carpet. He doesn't want us to criticize the worship leader; He wants us to pray for him or her. He doesn't want us to discuss how poor the leader's preaching is; He desires we intercede for the leader. God is going to raise up marvelous saints and leaders in houses of glory who are problem-solvers. They will implement strategic solutions in the areas of weakness around them.

FINDING FREEDOM

God the Father wants His sons and daughters to break agreement with the demonic spirits of accusation and fault-finding. He wants us to submit ourselves to the intercessory heart of Jesus Christ and a love that covers a multitude of sins. We must continually commit to cleaning out the filters of our hearts as we seek to minister the gifts of the Holy Spirit in love toward one another. Where there is accusation and fault-finding, the gifts of the Holy Spirit will not be exercised in true discernment and love. Is our heart to restore or hurt? Are we more easily given over to accusation and gossip or prayer and love for those who are struggling? Let us never lose sight of our own need for grace, mercy, and forgiveness. In the words of Jesus Christ: *"For if you for-give others for their transgressions, your heavenly Father will also forgive you. But if you do not forgive others, then your Father will not forgive your transgressions"* (Matt. 6:14-15).

NOTE

1. Francis Frangipane, *Exposing the Accuser of the Brethren* (Cedar Rapids, IA: Arrow Publications, 1991), 8-9.

Chapter 10

ITINERANT MINISTRY

*O*ne of the biggest problems within the fivefold ministry today is the number of itinerant ministers who spend little to no time at a home church. These traveling ministers are away too many weeks in a year and lose the ability to have meaningful, accountable relationships with a particular body of people. While many of them claim to have some kind of accountability, they lack weekly interaction with saints and local church leadership. This allows them the luxury of ministering to a corporate body on the weekends while they aren't actually immersed in a local church family themselves. Maybe they "attend" a church on occasion—when they are home. But there are no actual local church relationships for which they are responsible, and no mature elders to whom they are accountable. They are "too busy" for such biblical relationships, or they are too well-known to lower themselves to be part of a family with "normal" Christians. As we enter the new era, this paradigm for itinerant ministry must be confronted in love and done away with.

Every weekend, these traveling ministers speak at another conference or church. I personally had to learn that this lifestyle and schedule greatly damages the revelation fivefold ministers receive. It makes it impossible to have long-lasting fruit when ministering to a body of believers. Concerning these current trends among itinerant ministers, what does the New Testament have to say concerning traveling ministry? Is it possible that some merely "went" on their own initiative (see Jer. 23:21; 1 John 2:19) while others were truly "sent" with a divine assignment from above (see Acts 13:1-4; 1 Cor. 16:3, 6, 11; 2 Cor. 10:12-18)? Let's take a look at the Scriptures.

In John 12:49, Jesus said, *"For I did not speak on My own initiative, but the Father Himself who sent Me has given Me a commandment as to what to say and what to speak."* Jesus Christ came into the world under a divine commission from the Father and demonstrated a life of submission and surrender. In Matthew 8:5-13, Jesus approves of the faith of the Roman centurion who understood authority. Put simply, individuals can never carry more authority than they themselves are willing to submit to. The power and authority Jesus Christ walked in was directly connected to His submission to the will of the Father.

Following this same process and example, Jesus appoints seventy missionaries and commissions them to do the work of the Kingdom (see Luke 10:1-23). These were men who did not just travel and minster because they felt like it. Rather, they were sent out with a divine assignment to which they were accountable. Then as the New Testament Church gets established, the groundwork for further traveling ministry begins. At Antioch in Acts 13, the Holy Spirit says to set aside Paul and Barnabas for the work of apostolic ministry. Do these two men just pack their bags and leave, never to be heard of again? No! The whole church lays hands on them—after fasting and prayer!—and sends them out. Even after a direct, clear prophetic word from the Holy Spirit, the church still prayed and fasted to test the word and confirm the calling before sending out men who already functioned as prophets and teachers. The process was not rushed. It was nurtured carefully and prayerfully to make sure the sending was valid and all was in order. In the days ahead, these men would return to Antioch to give report of their time away and then go on mission again, both preaching the Gospel and visiting churches they planted as the Spirit led them. On his second missionary journey, Paul and his team remained in Corinth making disciples for a year and a half (see Acts 18:11). On his third missionary journey, Paul remained in Ephesus for three years doing the same (see Acts 20:31).

How do these New Testament examples of Jesus, Paul, and the other apostles compare to our modern-day itinerant ministries who have never had hands laid on them to be sent out, nor do they report back to home churches that supposedly sent them? These men are meant to be examples to the saints and fellow itinerant ministers (see 1 Cor. 4:6; 9:1-27). Notice also how Paul commended certain traveling ministers (see Rom. 16:1-2; 1 Cor. 16:10-12). And Luke presented the church in Antioch as a paradigmatic example as well.

THE TRAVELING DYSFUNCTION

After traveling and ministering all over the United States and world as a guest and conference speaker the last ten years, I would strongly estimate that at least 50 percent of the itinerant ministers who speak at churches and conferences *do not* attend a church consistently, are not immersed in a local body, and are not connected to its leadership. In fact, it's even more stunning how itinerant ministers respond when they are asked about this. "How can you minister to a body while you yourselves don't submit to, or enjoy true relationship with, your own local body?" Again, many of them claim to have a "home church" or a "pastor," but that's usually code word for: "I do not consistently attend or submit to local leadership anywhere." I, for one, believe this does incredible damage over time, not only to the Body of Christ, but to these itinerant ministers' spouses and families!

As they are on the road preaching at churches, they expect others to attend (or they would not have an audience or job), while they cannot find time to attend their own churches; their marriage and families are suffering from lack of relationship and community. Itinerant ministers and their families are, oddly, some of the most friendless individuals I have ever met, and it's incredibly sad. For all the lonely itinerant ministry wives and husbands, for all the itinerant ministry kids who will never experience the beauty and treasure of healthy community and accountability, I grieve with you. I have been an eyewitness to this destructive pattern and behavior with itinerant ministers over and over again. They are in desperate need of real Kingdom family.

DEMANDING TITLES AND HONORARIUMS

As a full-time church planter and itinerant minister of more than ten years, I have never once asked anyone to put a title in front of my name, nor have I required a specific honorarium when I come and minister. To many saints and leaders in the Body of Christ, this has completely shocked them—even angered a few—since, in their words, I have become "well-known."

Over the years as my influence increased, I sat down (or rather was sat down) by a well-known leader who chastised me for this behavior. "Jeremiah, you must begin to place a higher value on your gift, son. You have ministered and traveled the world, been on national radio and television, written books, and have an established ministry to the Body of Christ. If you do not start asking people to call you Apostle, or at least Prophet, Jeremiah, and require a specific honorarium when you travel, your influence will greatly diminish and people will no longer rightly assess and value what you are carrying," he said.

Tears began to well up in my eyes as I felt the Holy Spirit's deep grief over this man's counsel. I said to him, "Sir, with all due respect, our ministry receives over one hundred invitations per month for me to come minister and the size of the church, or what they can pay me, have never mattered. Ten people or 100,000 people, pay my own way or be accommodated, if God tells me to go, I'm going. No questions asked. I am a sent one, not a manipulated one—or a manipulating one."

His eyes about popped out of his head at this point. I continued, "As I've traveled the world these last ten years, I've received offerings well over ten thousand dollars, and I've received offerings that couldn't even cover my fuel to return home. I even minister at certain churches every year and purposely turn down their offerings and sow my own money into them." At this point, he began to become visibly upset with me.

I continued: "I planted a church ten years ago and have never even asked anyone to call me Pastor, Apostle, or Prophet. I like everyone just to call me Jeremiah. When God talks to me, He calls me 'Jeremiah,' and that's good enough for me. I will never charge an honorarium to come speak anywhere and I will never ask anyone to call me by any titles. I really don't like green rooms and entourages. I will always go where God tells me to go, and I believe He will always provide. I sow generously and God has blessed me generously. Thanks for your advice and counsel, but I just can't receive it." Livid and unwilling to even make eye contact again, he walked out of the room and has never talked to me again. I don't share this story to puff myself up in any way but rather to give the reader a real example of what is happening in parts of the Body of Christ today concerning itinerant ministry. We need to be seriously praying for those God has called to travel and bring His word to the saints and leaders.

I have a deep and unwavering conviction in my bones that God is raising up a generation of messengers who will refuse to charge for the Gospel no matter how influential they become. They will go by their first names, so that Jesus Christ might have preeminence in all things. If we have to demand people call us by a title, we probably don't carry the authority we claim to have anyway. If we have to demand people pay us certain, large amounts of money to come minister, we are simply being selfish—or may have a serious case of narcissism.

SEVEN KEYS FOR CHURCHES HOSTING ITINERANT MINISTERS

During my own experiences, both in hosting more than 100 itinerant ministers as well as preaching in more than 400 churches or conferences, I have come to learn seven keys I would highly recommend to all churches or ministries who host itinerant ministers.

These will save you potential misunderstanding, heartache, offense, bitterness, unforgiveness, and more. Say no to dysfunction!

1. *Work out logistics with itinerant ministers prior to their arrival.*

Do they expect a certain honorarium? If not, is there a ballpark figure that they usually receive when they minister so that you don't insult them when they leave? There are many traveling itinerant ministers with large ministries and varying scopes of influence who accept love offerings because they will not charge for the Gospel. While this is pure and right, please do not plan to give them a few hundred bucks for a series of weekend meetings and expect them to have all their needs met. They carry financial responsibilities for a ministry with greater needs than personal expenses. I highly recommend churches already have a built-in budget ready to bless them in case the offerings are way low.

Have you discussed whether you are going to pay for their travel to your city and food while they are there? Or should they assume that, if you give them $300 for the weekend, that might cover their gas or airfare and food? These are all issues and potential unnecessary sources of offense that should be covered before they come and minister. Also, please give them their honorarium or love offering *before* they leave. The more unanswered questions, the more likely misunderstanding will come in.

2. Never talk about your struggling church finances while they are present.

The fact that a church is struggling financially but still invites an itinerant minister to speak is almost always a red flag and warning sign that they are about to royally dishonor them. Traveling itinerant ministers are not magicians. A meeting or three with them cannot compensate for poor leadership around the clock—especially regarding finances. I have heard of one pastor who stole the itinerant minister's love offerings, saying he needed to take his family on vacation. If you as the host church or conference don't have enough money to bless itinerant ministers generously while they are with you, then you should not host them at all until you are able to bless them generously.

3. Never assume that they would love to stay with your deacon, elder, or staff member whom they've never met before.

Have you ever wanted to use the restroom, get comfortable, have freedom to do whatever you want and whenever you want, but couldn't because there were awkward restrictions put on you like being in a house with people you don't know or couldn't get comfortable around? The next time you host an itinerant minister, get him a nice hotel room and grant him the right to do whatever he wants and whenever he wants, outside of the meetings. You might be surprised that the meetings become much more fruitful this way!

4. Find out what their ministry styles are by asking them questions beforehand or inquiring about how they like to do altar ministry.

It can be awkward when an itinerant minister feels the anointing lift off the altar ministry and he is ready to go rest, when the host church leader is on a completely different page. It's a sad day when the host church leader continues to line people up to receive prayer and ministry when the itinerant minister is completely exhausted, worn out, and now feels like a prostitute. It's also a sad day when the itinerant minister does not give an altar call when the host church leader expected him too. These are all styles of ministry that can be dialogued through prior to services. Did you want the itinerant minister to preach on a certain subject? Why didn't you tell him?

5. Ask them what they like to eat and drink!

Don't assume that the itinerant ministers enjoy your cold potluck dinner after the meeting, and don't assume they are fasting like your church might be during that series of meetings. There's nothing better than a great meal after preaching to the point of exhaustion.

6. *Remember, they are human beings, not circus performers.*

Itinerant ministers have real issues and struggles like everyone else. They get tired, have families, and have to pay the bills too. Instead of focusing every minute of every conversation on you and your church, take some time to ask them how they are doing apart from any ministry. Trust me, this will form healthy relationships for years to come.

7. *If you announce to the crowds that* all *of the love offerings or honorariums will go to the itinerant minister, for the love of God and the sake of your integrity, do it!*

Don't use what people thought they were giving to the guest ministry to pay the church light bill, mortgage, your personal vacation, or any other nonsense. Also, always try your best to get them a check before they leave, not a month or two down the road. Many itinerant ministers constantly share stories of how they struggle week to week because they are not given their love offering in a reasonable amount of time.

Bonus

When seeking to book airfare for an itinerant minister, as long as he does not want first class (which, in my opinion, is an unreasonable expectation), be open to his booking his own ticket at a time that works best for him. Your church's need to save some more money, and therefore put them on a 6 A.M. flight or a late-night bogus flight, creates hardship for someone trying to spend more time with his family or already in the midst of an intense travel schedule. Remember—you want your guest speaker to be in top shape for your congregation, not survival mode. By taking care of traveling ministers, you are not just serving them—you are serving your congregation and yourself.

A RADICAL SHIFT TO ITINERANT MINISTRY

I see a radical shift coming to many itinerant ministries. Many of them are going to grow very weary of bringing temporary change to church communities on the weekend that they hardly know without ever investing in a community of believers whom they are in long-term love relationship with. Here are five more keys to healthy and successful itinerant ministry.

1. Itinerant ministers should be tested and sent by a local congregation, not merely

"called by God" and then invited as a public speaker (see Acts 13). If this is not the case, it takes away from the meaning and value of the visiting ministry. The spiritual failures below the surface will bear more bad fruit than the impact of gifts will impart on the surface. Popular speaking circuits are worldly; locally tested, proven, and sent ministries are authentic and meaningful. This applies to all kinds of fivefold ministers, because Saul and Barnabas in Acts 13 are examples to follow for all.

2. Qualifications for itinerants should be 1) *known* character—either from personal knowledge or real-life experience recommendations—as well as 2) authentic calling from the Lord. They should be proven fruit-bearers even if they are coming to have impact.

3. Develop long-term relationships with the local churches. Don't be a professional; be a servant with family values. But the nature of the relationship should be determined by the fivefold purpose of

the visits. No time to expound, but mentors should visit often, evangelists can boost outreach on occasion, apostles and prophets can invest, inject, help solve problems, etc. Everything should be relational and Spirit-led, not professional.

4. Be disciplined and purposeful. Popularity and numbers of invitations usually have nothing to do with God's call. Where is the Lord sending you? Why is He sending you there? Don't take invitations based on the popularity level of the church or the size of the conference. That's thinking professionally. Second Corinthians 4:2 kills that. Think biblically. Don't follow the money or numbers. That is shallow and has little impact (despite what it looks like). The Jesus principle of the "son of peace" should inform these kinds of decisions. One Samaritan woman was all that was needed for a whole city to get impacted (see John 4).

As we enter into a new era, it's not only going to impact what's happening inside houses of glory, but also those whom God is sending to minister to them.

Whether called to minister locally or trans-locally, houses of glory will no longer host performances or professional ministers. They will facilitate deep and authentic relationship between the fivefold ministry where the fullness of Jesus Christ can be manifested among fire, family, and fathering.

About Jeremiah Johnson

Jeremiah Johnson planted Heart of the Father Ministry in Lakeland, Florida in 2010 and served on the leadership team for a decade. In 2020, he moved his family to Charlotte, North Carolina to pursue a mandate to father and equip prophetic messengers. Jeremiah is a bestselling author of multiple books and travels extensively throughout the United States and abroad as a conference and guest speaker. He has been a guest on many popular Christian television and radio shows such as *Daystar, TBN, GOD TV,* Sid Roth: *It's Supernatural!,* and the *700 Club.* Jeremiah also enjoys hosting his own television show called *The Watchman's Corner.* For more go to: www.jeremiahjohnson.tv.

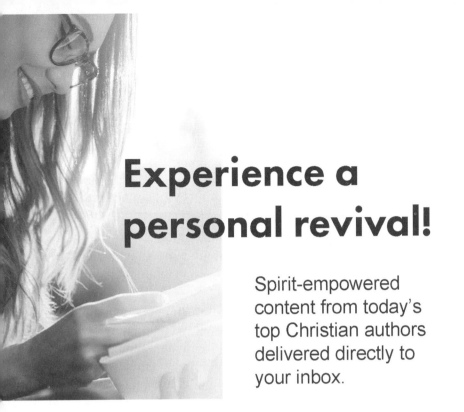

Experience a personal revival!

Spirit-empowered content from today's top Christian authors delivered directly to your inbox.

Join today!
lovetoreadclub.com

Inspiring Articles
Powerful Video Teaching
Resources for Revival

Get all of this and so much more, e-mailed to you twice weekly!

LOVE TO READ CLUB
by **D DESTINY IMAGE**